Series / Number 07-009

TIME SERIES ANALYSIS:
Regression Techniques

CHARLES W. OSTROM, JR.
Michigan State University

SAGE PUBLICATIONS / Beverly Hills / London

For information address:

SAGE PUBLICATIONS, INC.
275 South Beverly Drive
Beverly Hills, California 90212

SAGE PUBLICATIONS LTD
28 Banner Street
London EC1Y 8QE

International Standard Book Number 0-8039-0942-X

Library of Congress Catalog Card No. L.C. 77-93282

FIFTH PRINTING

When citing a professional paper, please use the proper form. Remember to cite the correct Sage University Paper series title and include the paper number. One of the two following formats can be adapted (depending on the style manual used):

(1) IVERSEN, GUDMUND R. and NORPOTH, HELMUT (1976) "Analysis of Variance." Sage University Paper series on Quantitative Applications in the Social Sciences, 07-001. Beverly Hills and London: Sage Pubns.

OR

(2) Iversen, Gudmund R. and Norpoth, Helmut. 1976. *Analysis of Variance.* Sage University Paper series on Quantitative Applications in the Social Sciences, series no. 07-001. Beverly Hills and London: Sage Publications.

CONTENTS

Editor's Introduction

Social scientists have become increasingly concerned with the analysis of change. Such an emphasis is the focus of TIME SERIES ANALYSIS, which examines techniques based on regression analysis for the study of change.* Many techniques are employed in the analysis of change, but regression analysis is the one most commonly employed and thus in the greatest need of a clear explication.

Research employing statistical methods will always have at least one of two fundamental types of data set: (1) *cross-sectional* data, in which the researcher has observations on a set of variables at a given point in time across many nations, states, counties, cities, or other units of analysis; or (2) *time-series* data, in which one has a set of observations on some variables for the same unit of analysis (such as a nation, state, etc.) over a series of time points (days, months, years, etc.). For either type of data, one can employ techniques based on regression analysis. Why, then, a special paper on regression techniques in TIME SERIES ANALYSIS?

The answer lies in the nature of time-series data. The regression model is based on a specific set of assumptions, relatively few in nature but very important if one is not to make erroneous inferences from the analysis of a data set. When we speak in terms of change over time, we may think of the analogy of "time's arrow," i.e., events in time move in one direction—forward. Social science data also move in one direction when examined over time in many cases. The world's population has been continually increasing over time; so has public spending by various units of government. When there is a general pattern of increases in the value of variables over time, however, some problems with regression estimation arise. In particular, it is likely that the assumption of independent error terms for succeeding observations may be

---

*See Herbert B. Asher (1976) *Causal Modeling,* in this series, for a discussion of the regression techniques and the assumptions behind the model, which Ostrom also presents in this paper.

violated. This is considerably less likely to occur in cross-sectional data analysis, where the order in which the observations are used to derive the regression estimates is rarely a matter of concern. Thus, one critical difference between cross-sectional analysis and TIME SERIES ANALYSIS is that, for the latter, it is critical that the data be processed in the order of the time periods involved. For yearly data, we enter 1952, 1953, 1954, 1955, 1956, etc. rather than 1955, 1952, 1954, 1956, etc. The way we process the data is important for two reasons: (1) the statistical properties of the regression estimators may be affected by the order in which we enter the cases, particularly if many of the variables are consistently increasing over time (or "tracking" like a missile, always in an upward direction);** and (2) as the author notes, TIME SERIES ANALYSIS allows us not only to get estimates of a regression equation, but also to make *forecasts* into the future from data in the past. If we were to order our data randomly, we might as well assume that the future can "come before" the past!

Charles W. Ostrom, Jr. demonstrates how regression techniques can be employed for both hypothesis testing and forecasting in TIME SERIES ANALYSIS. His major example concerns defense expenditures in the United States and the Soviet Union. This is a question that has interested students of politics, economics, and even applied mathematics throughout the twentieth century, with the earliest sophisticated statistical models developed by the applied mathematician Lewis Richardson.*** The subject of TIME SERIES ANALYSIS is important to all social scientists, however.

- Political scientists, in addition to studying changing patterns of expenditures on armaments and domestic social welfare programs (among other categories), have been concerned with changing patterns of party strength in presidential and congressional elections.

- Historians have studied electoral results over time, and examined changing patterns of migration and socioeconomic mobility in many societies, including the U.S. These studies often yield findings about social structures that have gone against the conventional wisdom of other scholars who relied exclusively on the writings of observers of previous eras rather than examining the available data on social structures. The growth of quantitative methods in history, together with a changing social consciousness, has led many historians to seek out data sources previously

---

**This terminology is taken from Ronald J. Wonnacott and Thomas H. Wonnacott (1970) *Econometrics.* New York: John Wiley.

***While Richardson did his work over a half century ago, the references in the international relations literature are all to two 1960 reprints: (1960a) *Arms and Insecurity* and (1960b) *Statistics of Deadly Quarrels,* both published in Chicago by Quadrangle Books.

thought unavailable, including census records of states and municipalities on the number and working conditions of slaves and freed slaves in nineteenth-century America.****

- Economists have been among the pioneers in developing TIME SERIES ANALYSIS (generally considered to be a branch of "econometrics," statistical methodology developed by economists). They have developed large-scale models of the economies of the U.S. and many other nations, with particular emphasis on changes over time and with forecasts of future trends.

- Sociologists have been concerned with many of the same demographic analyses from census tracts as historians. They also use TIME SERIES ANALYSIS to examine changes in life styles over generations, including questions of the differing roles for organized religion, sexual and racial characteristics, and values in types of behavior (such as family relations and individual voting choices).*****

- Psychologists and educators have examined changes in achievement levels of students. Are such changes related to the age of the student, changing racial and/or sexual roles, changes in curriculum or in the larger environment of the society (such as the amount of time spent watching television)?

What, then, is the scope of TIME SERIES ANALYSIS? Anything that moves! More appropriately, the answer should be anything subject to change. Thus, TIME SERIES ANALYSIS is fundamental to most of the questions posed in social science research. History is, after all, the study of change; the other social sciences merely examine what might be called "contemporary history." As Ostrom notes, the techniques discussed here provide an introduction to TIME SERIES ANALYSIS. Even within the regression framework, there are additional topics interested students should examine. Ostrom provides brief descriptions of these other techniques in a field where developments in statistical theory are constantly occurring. Thus the methodology, like the subjects of the analysis, is itself always changing.

—E. M. Uslaner, Series Editor

****A highly controversial work in this area, from both the perspective of the methods employed and the conclusions reached, is Robert W. Fogel and Stanley F. Engerman (1974), *Time on the Cross*. Boston: Little, Brown, and Co., in two volumes.

*****On generational change and how to distinguish it from other types of change, see Norval D. Glenn (1977) *Cohort Analysis* in this series.

TIME SERIES ANALYSIS:
Regression Techniques

CHARLES W. OSTROM, JR.
Michigan State University

1. INTRODUCTION

This monograph is designed to serve as an in-depth introduction to a variation of the basic regression model that utilizes data of a special type—time series. A collection of data X_t (t = 1, 2, . . . , T) with the interval between X_t and X_{t+1} being fixed and constant is referred to as a time series. In short, the order of the observations is of extreme importance—we are interested not only in the particular values of the observations but also in the order in which they appear. For example, series relating to U.S. defense expenditures, amount of war in the international system, presidential support, and unemployment meet the requirements of time series analysis. Thus, whereas in most treatments of regression (e.g., Wonnacott and Wonnacott, 1970; Kmenta, 1971; Johnston, 1972; Kelejian and Oates, 1974; Uslaner, 1978) the ordering of the observations has been irrelevant, in this paper it is of prime importance.

Given data that are in a specified temporal ordering, it is possible to raise questions concerning how the variable has behaved in the past and how it is likely to behave in the future. The great advantage of time series regression analysis is that it is possible to both explain the past and predict the future behavior of variables of interest. Thus the past history of a time series is called upon to do double duty (Nelson, 1973:19): "first, it must inform us about the particular mechanism which describes the evolution through time and second, it allows us to put that mechanism to use in forecasting the future." As can be seen, both of these efforts are predicated upon being able to correctly postulate a model and estimate its parameters. For example, the decision by the U.S. with respect to how much to spend for defense is of great concern to the President, Congress, the public, and other world leaders. As a result it is imperative that we try to understand how such a decision is made and what the future ramifications of the decision mechanism are likely to be. In an effort to provide some continuity to the technical discussion, we shall return to this example throughout this paper.

The discussion of time series regression analysis is divided into four parts. First, we discuss the general case by highlighting the problems and developing a procedure for correctly estimating time series regression models. Second, we focus on a modification of the procedure in which lagged values of the dependent or independent variables are included as explanatory variables. Third, methods of generating and evaluating forecasts from both types of models—lagged and nonlagged—using time series regression analysis are presented. Finally, some consideration is given to an advanced treatment of some of the topics which have been discussed in the three previous sections.

2. TIME SERIES REGRESSION ANALYSIS: NONLAGGED CASE

There are essentially two types of variables employed in regression analysis: endogenous and exogenous. An endogenous variable (usually denoted by a Y) is one whose values are explained by the model; it is often referred to as the dependent variable. Exogenous variables (usually denoted by a X) are those whose values are determined outside the confines of the present model; they are often called explanatory or independent variables. There are two basic types of time series regression models which employ these two types of variables: nonlagged and lagged. A nonlagged model concerns the relationship of variables over time in which both the endogenous and exogenous variables are observed at the same point in time. For example, we might hypothesize that current U.S. defense expenditures are related to current USSR defense expenditures. A lagged model, on the other hand, relates a current endogenous variable to past values of the exogenous and/or endogenous variables. That is, we might consider the relationship between the current U.S. defense spending and its past level plus current and lagged USSR spending levels. This section will focus on the nonlagged time series regression model.

A RATIO GOAL HYPOTHESIS

The search for an explanation of the rising pattern of U.S. defense expenditures over the past 25 years has led a number of scholars to try to specify models of the defense policymaking process (Ostrom, 1977). One of the possible explanations focuses on the U.S.'s reaction to the USSR's expenditure behavior. Such a model can be viewed as a ratio goal model and posits that U.S. defense expenditure levels are based on a desire to maintain some ratio of spending vis-à-vis the USSR. While there are other lines of reasoning which would lead to a similar conclusion, the basic hypothesis remains the same: the U.S. defense expenditure decision is based on the maintenance of fixed ratio relative to the USSR defense expenditure level.

The regression analog of this hypothesis can be stated as follows:

$$Y_t = a + b\,X_t + e_t \qquad [1]$$

where Y_t is the amount of money the U.S. spends on defense, X_t is the amount spent by the USSR, a is the grievance constant, b is the ratio goal, and e_t is a random disturbance term. Following Richardson (1960:16) the grievance constant is representative of a number of possible situations: if positive, it represents "deeply rooted prejudices, standing grievances, old unsatisfied ambitions [or] wicked and persistent dreams of world conquest"; and if negative, it represents "a permanent feeling of contentment." Therefore, even if the USSR does not spend anything, the U.S. may spend a fixed amount. The ratio goal, b, represents the defensive posture of the U.S. toward the USSR and will be less than 1.0 if the U.S. is willing to accept inferiority, equal to 1.0 if the U.S. desires parity, and greater than 1.0 if the U.S. demands superiority. If we compare this equation to the first equation in any basic treatment of regression analysis (e.g., Kmenta, 1971:201), we will notice that its form is identical to that in equation 1 except for the use of t as a subscript rather than i. The significance of this change is that time is now explicitly incorporated into the model.

To investigate the degree to which equation 1 accurately describes U.S. defense expenditure decisionmaking, we can apply simple regression to the U.S. and USSR defense expenditures data. For both historical and comparative purposes we shall refer to simple regression as Ordinary Least Squares (hereafter OLS) throughout the remainder of the paper. The results of the regression analysis are as follows:

$$Y_t = -9278 + 1.64\,X_t$$
$$(1.23)\quad(7.88)$$

$$R^2 = .82 \quad \text{s.e.} = \$6.05 \text{ billion}$$

where the numbers in parentheses are the t-ratios. As can be seen from the estimated version of equation 1, USSR defense expenditures have a strong positive impact on current U.S. spending. Furthermore, the U.S. demands clear superiority over the USSR, since b is substantially greater than 1.0. The interpretation of a is not quite so straightforward, however, because its t-ratio indicates that it is not significantly different from zero. Finally, the relationship as a whole accounts for 82 percent of the variance in Y_t. It appears that this version of the ratio goal hypothesis is supported by the data. Therefore, on the basis of prior theorizing, we expect the U.S. defense expenditure decision to be a function of USSR defense spending; the empirical results confirm this supposition.

There is a problem with this inference—the disturbance terms are not independent but instead are related to each other in a systematic manner. This makes any substantive conclusions tenuous at best. To overcome the problem and hence to estimate the model in an appropriate manner, we must be prepared to characterize the nature of the systematic relationship and then incorporate this information into the estimation procedure.

THE ERROR TERM

Of utmost importance to this and any other time series model is the error term. An error term is included in a model for one or more of the following reasons. First, given our desire to provide parsimonious explanations and because we cannot know all factors which are related to a given dependent variable, the usual practice is to recognize that some factors have been omitted from the equation. We have assumed, for example, that the USSR defense expenditure total is the sole determinant of U.S. defense spending. It is likely, however, that the previous level of U.S. spending, public opinion, unemployment, inflation, and the presence or absence of war all have an impact on the level of U.S. defense spending. A second source of error is related to the collection and measurement of data. This is a potential problem in the present context because of the problems associated with determining the level of spending in the USSR. A third source of error arises from the fact that "there is a basic and unpredictable element of randomness in human responses which can be adequately characterized only by the inclusion of a random variable term" (Johnston, 1972:11). These three factors are summarized by the error term, and we usually assume their effects are small and essentially random.

Given the presence of an error term, it is necessary to characterize the relationship between U.S. and USSR defense spending in stochastic terms. That is, for every X_t there exists a probability distribution of e_t's and therefore a probability distribution of Y_t's. Because of the probabilistic nature of the equation, the initial specification of the model must include some assumptions about the probability distribution of error terms. These are related to its mean, variance, and covariance. The following three assumptions are usually made:

(1) the error term has a mean of zero;

(2) the error term has a constant variance over all observations; and

(3) the error terms corresponding to different points in time are not correlated.

Of these, the third assumption is the most important. When the observations from different points in time are correlated, one of the assumptions is violated. When this occurs we say that the error process is *serially correlated* or *autocorrelated*. We will use these terms interchangeably throughout the paper.

The error term, e_t, cannot be observed and hence we will distinguish it from, $\hat{e}_t$, the residual or deviation of the dependent variable observation from its fitted value. Throughout the monograph the carat "∧" will be used to denote a parameter *estimate*. Errors are associated with the true regression model while residuals arise from the estimation procedure.

If the random factors in one period have no effect whatsoever on those in subsequent periods, we would expect to find a plot of residuals, $\hat{e}_t = Y_t - \hat{a} - \hat{b}X_t$, similar to Figure 1; that is, the observed residuals are randomly scattered around the regression life. If, on the other hand, the factors operating in one period carry over into the subsequent periods, we might find the residual plot similar to Figures 2 or 3.

If the U.S. spends a great deal of money for defense at time t so that $e_t > 0$, it might compensate in future time periods by reducing its expenditures at time t+1 to a level below the mean, so that $e_{t+1} < 0$. Note that this implies that the e_t and e_{t+1} are negatively correlated (i.e., high levels of the variable are followed by low levels). This type of behavior is depicted in Figure 2; if we were to plot the value of $\hat{e}_t$ over time, we would observe a pattern similar to that shown in Figure 4. Alternatively, values of the disturbance term could exhibit a positive correlation over time. For example, if there are factors at work which make it difficult for defense spending to be lowered immediately, we might observe that a positive value of e_t is typically followed by another positive value, and conversely. Assuming that the values of the disturbance term are in part determined by external forces

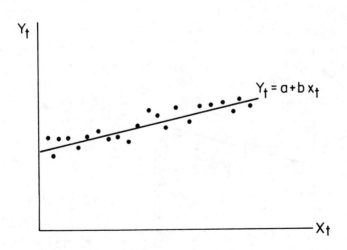

Figure 1: Randomly Scattered Residuals

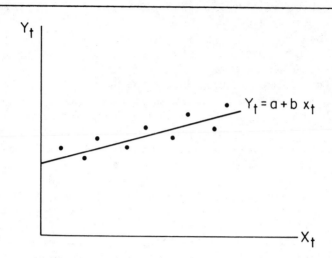

Figure 2: Negatively Autocorrelated Residuals

whose effects alternate between positive and negative, we might expect to find a number of runs of positive and negative signs. If it is difficult to lower defense spending once it rises, then above average amounts of spending $(e_t > 0)$ will be followed by above average amounts of spending $(e_{t+1} > 0)$; on the other hand, if there is a below average amount of spending $(e_t < 0)$,

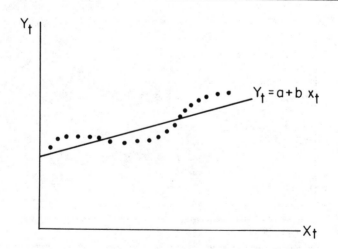

Figure 3: Positively Autocorrelated Residuals

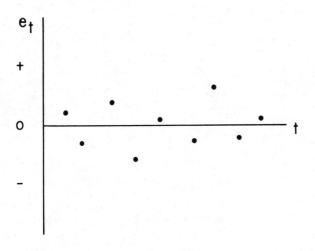

Figure 4: Negatively Autocorrelated Residuals Over Time

it may be difficult to get more money and hence there is likely to be a negative value of the following residual ($e_{t+1} < 0$). One such pattern is outlined in Figure 3 and its path through time is displayed in Figure 5.

To illustrate the argument to this point, the residuals from equation 1 have been plotted over time in Figure 6. As can be seen the pattern is very similar

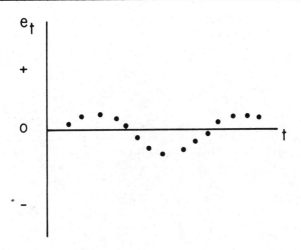

Figure 5: Postively Autocorrelated Residuals Over Time

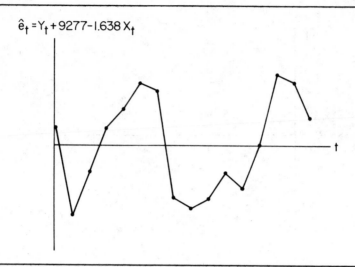

Figure 6: Estimated Residuals From Equation 1 Over Time

to that in Figure 5. It seems reasonable to conclude, therefore, that the residuals in equation 1 are not independent but instead exhibit positive serial correlation.

In order to be able to assess the consequences of autocorrelation, we must first specify the nature of the relationship between the error terms. One possible process, usually called a *first order autoregressive process*, can be formalized as follows:

$$e_t = pe_{t-1} + v_t \qquad [2]$$

where e_t is the error term at time t, e_{t-1} the error term at $t-1$, p is a regression coefficient, and v_t is a random variable with a zero mean, constant variance, and zero correlation with the other errors. Given the presence of first order autocorrelation (i.e., equations 1 and 2 are in effect), it can be shown that, while there is no effect on the parameter estimates (i.e., $\dot{a}$ and $\dot{b}$), there are problems with the estimated variances (i.e., var($\dot{a}$) and var($\dot{b}$)). Most regression computer programs routinely output estimates of the parameters and their variances. These are then used to generate the t-ratio,

$$t = \dot{b} / \sqrt{\text{var}(\dot{b})} \qquad \cdot$$

which is then used to assess the precision and significance of the individual estimates. Now, if the formulas used for the variances are no longer appropriate, the t-ratio is no longer valid. This creates problems for the investigator who wishes to test hypotheses relating to the strength and direction of the relationship between U.S. and USSR defense expenditure variables over time.

In our example there is evidence of positive serial correlation (i.e., $p > 0$ in equation 2). As we shall see shortly, this means that the estimated variances of a and b will be seriously underestimated. In the present case $p = .9$, which means that the usual formula for var ($\hat{b}$) will underestimate the true variance by as much as 900 percent, and hence the t-ratio will be inflated by approximately 300 percent. Thus it seems clear that we could be led to erroneously conclude that USSR spending has a significant influence on U.S. spending when there is significant autocorrelation. As a result, it is of considerable importance to test the null hypothesis that the estimated residuals are not mutually interdependent. The plot of the estimated residuals from equation 1 suggests that there is evidence of positive serial correlation. Obviously some correction needs to be introduced or the inferences concerning the goodness of fit of the model will lead us to erroneous conclusions.

Returning for a moment to the results from equation 1, it is clear that the simple regression results overestimate the "fit" of the model. If we were to ignore this overestimate we would be guilty of accepting the ratio goal model when, in fact, some other model might be true. In the statistical literature this is known as making a type II error. To avoid this problem, we need to formalize the relationship between the error terms and use that information to re-estimate the equation.

The purpose of this brief introduction has been to highlight the nature of the problem and provide some justification for studying autocorrelation. In the remainder of this section the assumptions underlying the regression model will be discussed. Special consideration is given to the nonautocorrelation assumption and its implications, the detection of its violation, the estimation of p, and the correction of the problems via a transformation of the data. Upon completion of the above topics we will return to equation 1 and suggest an appropriate approach to estimating a and b.

The major purpose of time series regression analysis is to make inferences, based on the estimated parameters, about the truth or falsity of a particular model. Given this orientation, it is very important that we keep the problem of serial correlation in mind. In a very real sense the analyst employing time series regression analysis faces a very difficult problem, namely that unless he has overwhelming amounts of information, it is impossible to make appropriate substantive inferences. However, failure to attempt a partial solution is likely to lead the same analyst to being overconfident about the substance and strength of his inferences. If such results are used to form the basis of policy recommendations this can have drastic consequences.

TIME SERIES REGRESSION MODEL

In the time series regression model, as in the general regression context, the time series analyst deals with stochastic relationships, that is, with those that include error terms in the specification of the model. The simplest form of such a model between two variables, say Y_t and X_t, is called the *simple time series regression model:*

$$Y_t = a + bX_t + e_t \qquad [3]$$

where Y_t is the endogenous variable, X_t is the exogenous variable, e_t is the random disturbance term, a and b are the unknown parameters, and the subscript t indicates that X_t and Y_t are a series of observations through time. The full specification of the simple time series regression model consists of the following basic assumptions (Pindyck and Rubinfeld, 1976:16-17):[1]

(1) Linearity: the relationship between Y and X is linear

(2) Nonstochastic X: $E[e_t X_t] = 0$

(3) Zero Mean: $E[e_t] = 0$

(4) Constant Variance: $E[e_t^2] = \sigma_e^2$

(5) Nonautoregression: $E[e_t e_{t-m}] = 0 \quad (m \neq 0)$

As can be seen, underlying the use of the time series regression model are a number of assumptions concerning the form of the model, the independent variable, and the disturbance terms.

Provided that these assumptions hold, it is possible to *optimally* estimate the regression parameters and their variances with the following formulas:

$$\hat{b} = \frac{\sum_{t=1}^{T} (X_t - \bar{X})(Y_t - \bar{Y})}{\sum_{t=1}^{T} (X_t - \bar{X})^2} \qquad [4]$$

$$\hat{a} = \bar{Y} - \hat{b}\bar{X}_t \qquad [5]$$

$$\mathrm{var}(\hat{b}) = s_e^2 / \sum_{t=1}^{T} (X_t - \bar{X})^2 \qquad [6]$$

$$\text{var}(\hat{a}) = s_e^2 \left[\frac{1}{T} + \frac{\bar{X}^2}{\displaystyle\sum_{t=1}^{T} (X_t - \bar{X})^2} \right] \qquad [7]$$

$$s_e^2 = \frac{\displaystyle\sum_{t=1}^{T} (Y_t - a - bX_t)}{T - 2} \qquad [8]$$

The estimators are optimal in the sense that they are unbiased, efficient, and consistent. Unbiased estimators are those in which the expected value of the estimator, say b, is equal to the true value, b. An estimator, say b, is relatively efficient if it has a smaller variance than any other estimator of b. An estimator will be consistent if both its bias and variance approach zero as the sample size approaches infinity. Together these properties mean that an estimator will be centered around the true value, have a relatively small dispersion, and will come increasingly close to the true value as the sample size increases. Assuming that the reader is familiar both with the derivation of the above estimation formulas and with the properties of unbiasedness, relative efficiency, and consistency (if not, please consult a discussion of regression such as Uslaner, 1978; or Pindyck and Rubinfeld, 1976:21-24), we will focus our attention on the problems created by the violation of the non-autoregression assumption.

The five assumptions elucidated earlier constitute the classical linear regression model. By adding the following assumption, we have the classical normal linear regression model (Pindyck and Rubinfeld, 1976:20):

(6) Normality: the error term is normally distributed

This assumption is necessary only for the statistical testing of the model (e.g., significance tests such as t-test). As Pindyck and Rubinfeld (1976:20) note, as long as "one is willing to believe that the individual errors due to measurement and to omission are small and independent of each other, then the normality assumption is a reasonable one." This assumption will allow us to derive significance tests and confidence intervals for the regression coefficients. As Johnston (1972:135) points out, it is also possible to make no explicit assumption about the form of the distribution and to appeal instead to the Central Limit Theorem to justify the use of the usual tests. Even though the normality assumption is not crucial to most of the subsequent development, it is necessary to understand the role of this assumption in the inference process. Interested readers should consult Christ (1966:513, 521) for a test of the normality assumption and a discussion of the implications of its violation.

NONAUTOREGRESSION ASSUMPTION

While each of the assumptions is necessary to establish certain properties of the simple regression estimators, of special importance are the three error term assumptions (assumptions 3, 4, and 5). Of particular interest are assumptions 3 and 5, which together, imply that the covariance of any two disturbance terms (i.e., $cov(e_t e_{t-m})$) is equal to zero. This can be seen as follows:

$$
\begin{aligned}
cov(e_t e_{t-m}) &= E\,[e_t - E(e_t)]\,\,[e_{t-m} - E(e_{t-m})] \\[6pt]
&= E\,[e_t - 0]\,\,[e_{t-m} - 0] \\[6pt]
&= E\,[e_t e_{t-m}] \\[6pt]
&= 0
\end{aligned}
\tag{9}
$$

This means that we are assuming that disturbances at one point in time are not correlated with any other disturbances. When this assumption holds, equations 4, 5, 6, 7, and 8 represent the appropriate estimating formulas. When this assumption is violated, however, equations 6, 7, and 8 are no longer appropriate.

To formalize our reasoning, let us assume that the dependence between the error terms takes the form of a first order autoregressive process (i.e., equation 2):

$$
\begin{aligned}
&e_t = p e_{t-1} + v_t \\[6pt]
&E\,[v_t] = 0 && \text{for all t} \\[6pt]
&E\,[v_t^2] = \sigma_v^2 && \text{for all t} \\[6pt]
&E\,[v_t v_{t-m}] = 0 && m \neq 0, \text{ for all t} \\[6pt]
&E\,[v_t e_{t-1}] = 0 && \text{for all t} \\[6pt]
&-1 < p < +1
\end{aligned}
\tag{10}
$$

Making these assumptions suggests that any disturbance is related to its immediately preceding value by a simple linear regression model; each disturbance is equal to a portion (since p is less than 1.0 in absolute value) of the preceding disturbance term plus a random variable. By successive substitution for $e_{t-1}, e_{t-2}, \ldots$ in equation 2, we obtain the following:

$$e_t = pe_{t-1} + v_t$$

$$= p[pe_{t-2} + v_{t-1}] + v_t$$

$$\cdot$$
$$\cdot$$
$$\cdot$$

$$= p^m e_{t-m} + p^{m-1} v_{t-m+1} + \ldots + pv_{t-1} + v_t \qquad [11]$$

$$\cdot$$
$$\cdot$$
$$\cdot$$

$$= p^t e_0 + p^{t-1} v_1 + p^{t-2} v_2 + \ldots + pv_{t-1} + v_t \qquad [12]$$

This shows that each disturbance, e_t, is generated as a linear function of the random effects $v_1, v_2, \ldots, v_t$ and of the initial disturbance term, e_0 (Kmenta, 1971:271). Having already specified the manner in which the v_t's are generated, it is now necessary to specify the process generating the initial value of e, e_0. As Kmenta (1971:271) notes, the following characterization is useful:

$$E[e_0] = 0$$
$$E[e_0^2] = \sigma_v^2 / 1-p^2 \qquad [13]$$

That is, the initial disturbance has a zero mean and a constant variance.

Based upon the characterization in equation 12, we can inquire whether a disturbance term which follows the first order autoregressive process violates any of the basic assumptions. First,

$$E[e_t] = p^t E[e_0] + p^{t-1} E[v_1] + \ldots + E[v_t]$$
$$= 0 \qquad [14]$$

since all of the random variables have expected values of zero. Thus the expected value of the disturbance term is zero. Next, note that the constant variance assumption is not violated (Kmenta, 1971:272):

$$\text{var}(e_t) = (p^t)^2 \text{var}(e_0) + (p^{t-1})^2 \text{var}(v_1) + \ldots \text{var}(v_t)$$

$$= p^{2t} [\sigma_v^2 / 1-p^2] + p^{2(t-1)} \sigma_v^2 + \ldots + p^2 \sigma_v^2 + \sigma_v^2$$

$$= p^{2t} [\sigma_v^2 / 1-p^2] + \sigma_v^2 [p^{2(t-1)} + p^{2(t-2)} + \ldots + p^2 + 1]$$

$$= \sigma_v^2 [p^{2t} / 1-p^2 + 1-p^{2t} / 1-p^2] \qquad [15]$$

$$= \sigma_v^2 / 1-p^2$$

Thus all of the e's have the same variance. Note the ramifications of violating the assumption that p must be less than 1.0 in absolute value; if p is equal to 1.0, the variance of e_t would be infinite and any Y_t that is observed could be completely dominated by the explosive error term (Wonnacott and Wonnacott, 1970:141).

Finally, to examine the covariance of disturbance terms, let us multiply equation 11 by e_{t-m} and take the expected value:

$$E[e_t e_{t-m}] = p^m E(e_{t-m}^2) + p^{m-1} E(e_{t-m} v_{t-m+1}) + \ldots +$$

$$p E(e_{t-m} v_{t-1}) + E(e_{t-m} v_t)$$

$$= p^m var(e_{t-m})$$

$$= p^m \sigma_e^2$$

[16]

So long as p is nonzero, the covariance is nonzero and hence one of the basic assumptions is violated. Thus, if the error term follows the pattern noted in equation 10, all the assumptions but one remain satisfied. The exception is that the nonautoregression assumption does not hold.

To see what equation 10 implies, it is instructive to consider the auto-correlation function, which portrays the correlation of the error terms at different points in time. The autocorrelation function of error terms j periods apart, A_j, is defined as follows:

$$A_j = \frac{cov[e_t e_{t-j}]}{\sqrt{var[e_t]} \; \sqrt{var[e_{t-j}]}}$$

[17]

for j=1, 2, . . . By substitution this becomes

$$A_j = p^j \sigma^2 / \sigma^2$$

because the e's have a constant variance and because the covariance has been derived in equation 16. This reduces to

$$A_j = p^j$$

[18]

This is an important result because it describes theoretically the correlation of the disturbances j periods apart when they are generated by a first order autoregressive process. Notice that the autocorrelation function is the correlation coefficient between the disturbances, and hence its values range from -1 to $+1$. This means that p is the coefficient of correlation between e_t and

e_{t-1}, p^2 is the coefficient of correlation between e_t and e_{t-2}, p^3 is the coefficient of correlation between e_t and e_{t-3}, and so on. Furthermore, $p = +1$ or -1 is ruled out by assumption. Finally, whenever $p = 0$, we have

$$e_t = v_t$$

$$\text{var}[e_t] = \sigma_v^2$$

$$\text{var}[e_0] = \sigma_v^2$$

and because the e's have a zero mean and a constant variance, all of the basic assumptions hold.

Thus a basic indicator of whether the nonautoregression assumption is violated is whether there is a sample correlation between the various random disturbance terms; no other assumptions are involved. To obtain a visual indication of the nature of the correlation, it is helpful to construct a correlogram which provides a graphical representation of the estimated autocorrelation function, with time lags (j) and autocorrelation coefficients (A_j) forming the axes. Figures 7 and 8 illustrate two hypothetical cases. Note that when there is positive autocorrelation (see Figure 7) the correlations damp off smoothly and exponentially, whereas negative autocorrelation (see Figure 8) produces an oscillatory and exponential decay of successive correlations.

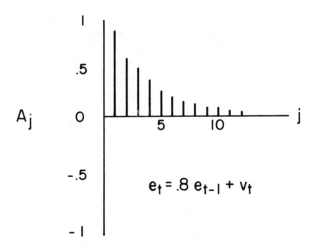

Figure 7: Theoretical Correlogram for First Order Process, p = +.8

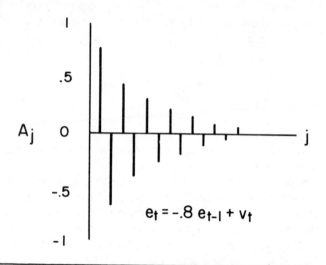

Figure 8: Theoretical Correlogram for First Order Process, p = −.8

To this point, we have examined the basic assumptions of the regression model and have focused on the nonautoregression assumption because of its appropriateness to the time series context. The problem arises in time series analysis because the disturbances, which are a summary of a large number of theoretically irrelevant (and supposedly random) factors that enter into the relationship under study, are likely to carry over into subsequent time periods. In this regard Kmenta likens the autoregressive disturbance to the sound effect of tapping a musical instrument (Kmenta, 1971:270):

> while the sound is loudest at the time of impact, it does not stop immediately but lingers on for a time until it finally dies out. This may also be characteristic of the disturbance, since its effect may linger for some time after its occurence. But while the effect of one disturbance lingers on, other disturbances take place, as if the musical string were tapped over and over, sometimes harder than at other times.

This analogy is consistent with the presence of a first order autoregressive process discussed in this section.

Virtually all work in time series regression analysis assumes that a first order autoregressive process is generating the disturbances. While not the only process possible, the first order autoregressive process is studied so often because of its statistical tractibility and because it yields a crude approximation to the processes in which we are interested. Having developed the implications of the violation of the nonautoregression assumption, it is appropriate to turn to a consideration of the consequences of such a violation.

CONSEQUENCES OF VIOLATING THE
NONAUTOREGRESSION ASSUMPTION

Before presenting the formal consequences of violating the nonautoregression assumption it is useful to consider the following example presented by Wonnacott and Wonnacott (1970:136-140). They posit the following very simple model:

$$Y_t = a + bX_t + e_t$$

$$e_t = e_{t-1} + v_t \qquad [19]$$

$$X_t = X_{t-1} + u_t$$

where v_t satisfies assumptions 3, 4, and 5. Notice that both e_t and X_t are assumed to be autoregressive, with X_t being assumed to increase over time regularly (i.e., $E(u_t) > 0$). Wonnacott and Wonnacott perform a simple experiment in which they generate e_t and X_t that conform to the above specifications and then compute Y_t. OLS is then applied to simulated data to see what happens to a and b when the nonautoregression assumption is violated and the X_t are increasing over time.

To illustrate what happens, Wonnacott and Wonnacott draw a sample of 20 independent values of v_t and, starting with $e_0 = 5$, generate $e_1, e_2, \ldots,$ e_{20}. The comparison between the random v_t and the autocorrelated e_t is shown in Figure 9. It is clear that the autocorrelation is positive, because e_t tends to be positive when e_{t-1} is positive, and negative when e_{t-1} is negative. Figure 10 presents the true and estimated regression lines along with the true and estimated e_t's. Studying Figure 10 indicates the difficulties created by serial correlation—a is underestimated and b is overestimated. If the order of the residuals were reversed, however, so that they were negative first and then positive, b would be underestimated and a overestimated. As a result there does not appear to be a problem with bias: because b is as likely to be overestimated as underestimated, it will on the average be equal to the true value.

Clearly there is a substantial difference between the true and estimated error terms in Figure 10, and this is the source of the problem created by autocorrelation. The reasons for the problem can be seen by comparing the serial correlation of Figure 10 with an identical model with no serial correlation presented in Figure 11. The figures are alike in all respects (note especially that the error variances are identical), except that one model exhibits

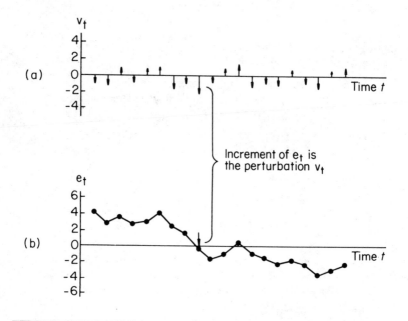

Figure 9: The Construction of a Serially Correlated Error Term. (a) Independent Perturbation v_t. (b) Generated Error: $e_t = e_{t-1} + v_t$

serial correlation and the other does not. While the estimated residuals in Figure 11 are very similar to the actual residuals, the estimated residuals in Figure 10 are not at all similar to the true, autocorrelated residuals. The reasons for this should be quite clear—the line in Figure 10 is fit under the assumption that the error terms are not autocorrelated. The result is that the error variance will be seriously underestimated; the regression line appears to fit the data much more accurately than it actually does.

The implication of this result is that in the presence of autocorrelated residuals the estimated regression line fits the data quite well, leaving the small estimated residuals shown in Figure 10. Thus the estimated variances will seriously underestimate the true variances. Furthermore, as Uslaner (1978) shows, the estimated variances are extremely important in constructing confidence intervals, testing hypotheses, and computing t-ratios. In the presence of serially correlated errors we are likely to be led to the paradoxical result that even though the estimated coefficients appear quite reliable (small variances) they are in fact extremely unreliable.

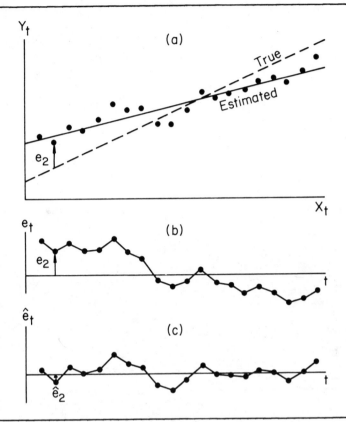

Figure 10: Regression with Serially Correlated Error. (a) True and Estimated regression lines. (b) True error terms. (c) Estimated error terms

Source: Wonnacott and Wonnacott (1970, p. 138).

The reasons for the experimental results obtained by Wonnacott and Wonnacott can be seen by considering the more general form of their simple model:

$$Y_t = a + bX_t + e_t$$

$$e_t = pe_{t-1} + v_t$$

$$X_t = cX_{t-1} + u_t \qquad [20]$$

$$-1 < p < +1$$

$$-1 < c < +1$$

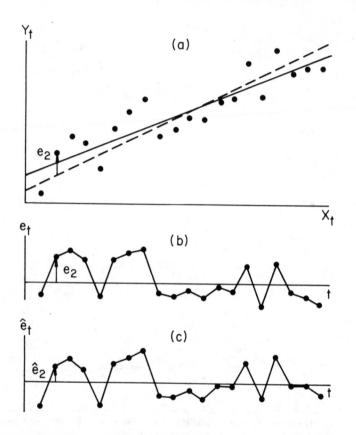

Figure 11: Regression with Independent Error (yet same variance as in Figure 10).
(a) True and Estimated regression lines. (b) True error terms. (c) Estimated error terms

Source: Wonnacott and Wonnacott (1970, p. 139).

Johnston (1972:247) has shown that the general formula for the variance of b is

$$\text{var}(b) = \frac{\sigma^2}{\Sigma(X_t - \bar{X})^2} \left[\frac{1 + pc}{1 - pc} \right] \qquad [21]$$

Based upon the above result, we can calculate the bias in the estimated variance given a value of p and c. Equation 21 also suggests a way to compute the bias in the estimated t-ratios:

$$t = b / \sqrt{\mathrm{var}(b)} = \sqrt{\frac{1 - pc}{1 + pc}} \left[\frac{b}{\sigma / \sqrt{\sum_t (X_t - \bar{X})^2}} \right] \qquad [22]$$

Thus if $c = p = .9$, $(1 + .81)/(1 - .81) = 9.53$, so that the true variance is underestimated by 953 percent. Furthermore, $\sqrt{(1 - .81)/(1 + .81)} = .32$, which means that the true t-ratio is overestimated by 309 percent. Thus if we were to engage in a hypothesis test using the t-ratio, the results would be very biased towards rejecting the null hypothesis of no effect. This could in turn lead to considerable overconfidence in the strength of our results in the presence of strong positive serial correlation.

Moreover, the situation is likely to be much worse than this example suggests. This is because there may well be a bias in the estimated variance, s^2. In fact the OLS residuals are likely to underestimate σ^2 when the e's are autocorrelated. As Johnston (1972:249) shows,

$$E[s^2] = \sigma^2 \left[T - \frac{1 + pc}{1 - pc} \right] \qquad [23]$$

so that, if $p = c = .9$ and $T = 16$, there is an underestimation of 57 percent. The two biases work in the same direction so that, in the case of the model with autocorrelated errors, the simple OLS formula for the variance (equation 8) will further bias the estimates of the coefficient variances (equations 6 and 7). Note that this component is likely to become less significant as the sample size becomes larger.

Table 1 reproduces the results of an experiment by Malinvaud (1970:522) in which he presents the bias in $\hat{a}$ and $\hat{b}$ for various values of p and c and which includes the contribution of s^2. Notice that when there is no autoregression in the X_t's (i.e., $c = 0$), the bias in b is small even if the p is large. This is not very comforting, however, because as Malinvaud (1970:522) notes:

> most of the quantities introduced as exogenous variables have fairly smooth evolutions. They are generally high autocorrelated. We must therefore bear in mind that *the usual formulae seriously overestimate the precision of the estimates whenever there is considerable serial correlation of errors.*

Finally, it should be noted that in most political and economic data the serial correlation is likely to be positive, because the same random factors tend to operate on at least two successive periods' errors (and likely on

TABLE 1
Estimates of a and b for Various Values of p and c

Autocorrelation of the errors(p)	Autocorrelation of the exogenous variable (c)				
	−.4	0	.4	.6	.8
	coefficient b relating to the slope				
−.4	1.4	1	.7	.6	.5
0	1.0	1	1.0	1.0	1.0
.4	.8	1.1	1.5	1.8	2.1
.6	.8	1.2	1.9	2.6	3.6
.8	1.2	1.7	3.4	6.0	11.0
	coefficient a relating to the intercept				
−.4	.4	.4	.4	.4	.5
0	1.0	1.0	1.0	1.0	1.0
.4	2.5	2.5	2.5	2.5	2.6
.6	4.6	4.7	4.8	4.8	5.0
.8	14.0	15.0	16.0	18.0	22.0

Source: Malinvaud (1970, p. 522).

more). Hence we should be wary of the possibility of positive serial correlation in both the error terms and the independent variables.

Thus when disturbances are autoregressive the conventional formulas for carrying out hypothesis tests and/or constructing confidence intervals are likely to lead to incorrect inferences. Furthermore, because the autocorrelation is likely to be positive, the calculated acceptance regions or confidence bounds may well be much narrower than the true regions or bounds. Hence one can erroneously conclude that a variable exerts a significant causal influence if the model in question exhibits positive serial correlation. Hibbs (1974:259) argues that the effects of autocorrelation are likely to be even more pernicious than this:

Nevertheless OLS regression in the presence of serially correlated disturbances is not necessarily disastrous. . . . After all, the parameter estimates are unbiased. More problematic and more typical, however, is the situation where the researcher analyzes many equations in the process of evaluating competing hypotheses and equally plausible alternative functional forms. Given the characteristic collinearity of independent variables in such studies, the erroneous selection of variables or entire equations because of differential bias in t- and F-statistics can seriously impair the causal inference-model building process. In time-series analyses of this sort, it is clear that autocorrelation is no longer a comparatively minor problem of estimation precision: if the sequential development of complex multivariate models is grounded on biased and unreliable decision rules, errors of inference may cumulate and far exceed those that arise in a single analysis of a single equation.

Autocorrelation can indeed have an important impact on the quality of the inferences we draw from our empirical analyses.

CONVENTIONAL TESTS FOR AUTOCORRELATION

Since autocorrelation poses such serious problems for the use of simple OLS, it is extremely important to test for its presence in a given sample. If we do not know or are not willing to assume that the error in question is or is not autoregressive, we must turn to the sample for information. In particular we wish to test the hypothesis that

$$H_o: \; p = 0$$

against the alternative

$$H_A: \; p > 0$$

The latter is chosen because the previous discussion suggests that positive autocorrelation is by far the most likely occurrence. Since negative autocorrelation may occur, however, we will also discuss tests for it.

For large samples, we have the choice of a number of tests which can be applied to the residuals computed from the OLS regression (i.e., $\hat{e}_t = Y_t - \hat{a} - \hat{b}X_t$). The basic question to be answered by the test is whether the estimated residuals are random. Available tests are of two types (Johnston, 1972:250): (1) distribution-free tests, and (2) tests based on theoretical distributions. Although the latter tests are more widely used, they can be computationally quite burdensome if the appropriate computer program is not available. Therefore, we will investigate an available distribution-free test, which requires nothing more than a listing of the estimated residuals.

One possible distribution-free test is called the Geary test (Habibagahi and Pratschke, 1972:184), which provides a simple, quick, and easy method for testing for autocorrelation without having to have recourse to the computations required for the Durbin-Watson." The Geary test involves a simple count of sign changes in the regression residuals. Habibagahi and Pratschke (1972) show the probability of r sign changes and provide a handy reference table of critical values at the .05 and .01 levels for 3 to 55 cases. The test involves computing a minimum and maximum number of runs in order to test the null hypotheses of no positive or no negative autocorrelation. If there is positive serial correlation (see Figure 3) we would expect very few sign changes, whereas if there is negative serial correlation (see Figure 2) we would expect a large number of sign changes. Thus to test for serial correlation we first compute the regression, estimate the residuals, and count the sign changes; we then compare this number to the minimum and maximum values to determine whether there is significant positive or negative autocorrelation.

The Geary test is not as powerful as one based on a theoretical distribution, but it is easy to compute since it requires so little information. This test becomes much more useful for large sample sizes (i.e., $n > 30$). Finally the test not only provides interesting information regarding the presence or absence of significant serial correlation but also helps us understand what the problem entails in terms of sign changes.

As can be seen in Figure 6, there are four sign changes in the residuals from equation 1. The minimum and maximum number of sign changes for the Geary test at the .01 and .05 levels respectively are 3, 11 and 4, 10. Based on this test there is reason to accept the null hypothesis of no serial correlation. However, because these results conflict with those which will be discussed in the next few pages, it is important to keep in mind that the Geary test is not very powerful in samples as small as the one in Figure 6.

Turning now to a test based on a theoretical distribution, we shall focus on the Durbin-Watson d-statistic:

$$d = \frac{\sum_t (\dot{e}_t - \dot{e}_{t-1})^2}{\sum_t \dot{e}_t^2} \qquad [24]$$

where the $\dot{e}_t$'s are the OLS regression residuals. It should be clear that, when there is positive autocorrelation, the value of the numerator (i.e., $\dot{e}_t - \dot{e}_{t-1}$) will be small relative to the value of the denominator, while for negative autocorrelation the opposite will be the case. Thus d will tend to be small for positive autocorrelation, large for negative autocorrelation, and somewhere in the middle for a random series.

As a generalization of equation 24 it follows, if we assume $e_t = pe_{t-1} + v_t$, that (Kelejian and Oates, 1974:202):

$$d = \frac{2 \, \text{var}(\hat{e}_t) - 2 \, \text{cov}(\hat{e}_t \hat{e}_{t-1})}{\text{var}(\hat{e}_t)}$$

which, based on previous results, is

$$= \frac{2s^2 - 2ps^2}{s^2}$$

$$= 2(1-p)$$

[25]

This suggests, in turn, that

$$p = 0 \quad \text{implies } d = 2$$
$$p = -1 \quad \text{implies } d = 4$$
$$p = 1 \quad \text{implies } d = 0$$

It should be stressed that these are only approximations, since the sampling distribution of the Durbin-Watson depends upon the specific values of the X_t's. As a result, Durbin and Watson established upper (d_u) and lower (d_l) limits for the significance levels of d. These allow us to test the hypothesis of no autocorrelation against the alternative hypothesis of positive first order autocorrelation. The decision rule in the case of positive serial correlation is (Kmenta, 1971:295):

$$\text{if } d < d_l \quad \text{reject } H_0$$
$$d_u < d < 4 - d_u \quad \text{do not reject } H_0$$
$$d_l \leqslant d \leqslant d_u \quad \text{inconclusive}$$

If the hypothesis is negative first order serial correlation, the decision rule becomes (Kmenta, 1971:295):

$$\text{if } 4 - d_l < d \quad \text{reject } H_0$$
$$d_u < d < 4 - d_u \quad \text{do not reject } H_0$$
$$4 - d_u \leqslant d \leqslant 4 - d_l \quad \text{inconclusive}$$

A diagrammatic representation of these decision rules is given in Figure 12.

The inconclusive region is a range of values in which we can neither accept nor reject the null hypothesis—in short, we can draw no inferences. This presents a problem when using the Durbin-Watson test. Theil and Nagar (1961) offer a partial solution based upon more specific assumptions about the exogenous variables. Their assumptions concern the first and second differences of the exogenous variables—they must be small in terms of the

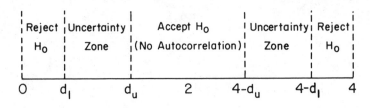

Figure 12: Five Regions for Values of Durbin-Watson d
Source: Kelejian and Oates (1974, p. 202).

original variables. Thus variables with a trend qualify, but data expressed in first differences do not. The Theil and Nagar values are computed as follows:

$$.01 \text{ level:} \quad Q = 2 \left[\frac{T-1}{T-k} - \frac{2.32635}{\sqrt{T+2}} \right]$$

[26]

$$.05 \text{ level:} \quad Q = 2 \left[\frac{T-1}{T-k} - \frac{1.64485}{\sqrt{T+2}} \right]$$

The Theil-Nagar Q-values are very close to the Durbin-Watson d_u's, so that common practice simply uses the upper limit as the cut-off point. This causes the null hypothesis to be rejected even if the value of d is in the inconclusive region.

What action, if any, should be taken in response to the outcome of a test for the presence of serial correlation? If there is no indication of significant serial correlation, we can accept the OLS estimates without fearing a loss of efficiency or a bias in the estimated variances. If there is an indication of significant autocorrelation, there is some reason to be concerned: one response might be to use the estimation techniques developed in the next two sections. Finally, if the test is inconclusive, we may or may not respond. Given the seriousness of the consequences, however, we can adopt the Theil and Nagar levels (or simply use d_u) and take corrective action any time there is an indication of significant serial correlation.

In closing, there are three related points which need to be emphasized. First, it must be stressed that the Durbin-Watson test is not valid if one or more of the regressors are lagged endogenous (i.e., dependent) variables (Nerlove and Wallis, 1966). We shall return to the reasons for this in the next major section of the paper. Second, Griliches and Rao (1969) note, on the basis of Monte Carlo experiments, that when the disturbance is generated by a first order autoregressive process and $p > .30$, the alternative estimation techniques (developed in the next two sections) should be used in place of OLS. Consequently Hibbs (1974), among others, finds $p > .30$ a more appealing rule of thumb than either the Durbin-Watson or Theil-Nagar levels. Finally, if the regression model in question has more than one exogenous variable, the Durbin-Watson d-statistic requires knowledge of the number of regressors. Durbin and Watson have computed values of d for $k = 1, 2, 3, 4, 5$. It is also necessary to note whether k includes or specifically excludes the constant term in its count. A safe strategy is to assume that k includes the constant term unless it is otherwise stated.

The Durbin-Watson d-statistic for the estimated version of equation 1 is .89. To determine whether this value is consistent with the null hypothesis of no positive serial correlation, it is necessary to determine d_u and d_l for $T = 16$ and $k = 2$. Looking at a standard table yields the following lower and upper bounds for the .05 level: .98 and 1.24. Because d is less than the lower bound, it is clear from Figure 11 that we must reject the null hypothesis. Had we used the .01 level, the lower and upper bounds would be .84 and 1.09, so that d would lie in the inconclusive region. When faced with the problems created by this situation it is usually appropriate to compute the Theil-Nagar bounds (see equation 26), which are 1.04 and 1.36 for the .01 and .05 significance levels respectively. Using the Theil-Nagar levels we can therefore clearly reject the null hypothesis of no serial correlation at both the .01 and .05 levels. These test results confirm our suspicion that the plotted residuals from Figure 6 exhibit positive serial correlation.

AN ALTERNATIVE METHOD OF ESTIMATION

Kelejian and Oates (1974:195) provide the following general summary of the problem of autocorrelation:

> The general character of the problem of autocorrelation should now be clear. Where it is present, we have a systematic variation in the values of the disturbance term for successive observations. This pattern of variation does not lead to biased estimates of the parameters; however, the variance formulas no longer hold and consequently, without further results we would be unable to test hypotheses and establish confidence intervals. Our procedure obviously leaves something to be desired. . . . If there is a pattern to the variation among the disturbance terms, we should be able to do a better job of estimation and prediction if we incorporate this additional information into our calculations.

To do so, let us return to the basic model which we have been considering:

$$Y_t = a + bX_t + e_t$$
$$e_t = pe_{t-1} + v_t$$
$$-1 < p < +1$$
$$E[v_t] = 0 \quad E[v_t^2] = \sigma^2$$

[27]

We will assume, furthermore, that p is known. Now take a lagged form of equation 27 and multiply it through by p to obtain:

$$pY_{t-1} = pa + pbX_{t-1} + pe_{t-1}$$

[28]

Subtracting equation 28 from equation 27 yields:

$$(Y_t - pY_{t-1}) = (a - ap) + (bX_t - pbX_{t-1}) + (e_t - pe_{t-1})$$

[29]

From equation 27 we know that $v_t = e_t - pe_{t-1}$, which when substituted into equation 29 gives:

$$(Y_t - pY_{t-1}) = a(1-p) + b(X_t - pX_{t-1}) + v_t$$

or

$$Y'_t = a' + bX'_t + v_t$$

[30]

where

$$Y'_t = Y_t - pY_{t-1}$$
$$X'_t = X_t - PX_{t-1}$$
$$a' = a(1-p)$$

Note that the number of observations is reduced by one when employing this transformation, since data does not usually exist for Y_0 and X_0.

Equation 30 is now in standard regression format—in particular, v_t satisfies all of the basic assumptions (unlike e_t). Applying OLS to equation 30 yields the following estimates for $\hat{a}$, $\hat{b}$, var($\hat{a}$), and var($\hat{b}$):

$$\hat{a} = (1/1-p) \, [\bar{Y}'_t - \hat{b}\bar{X}'_t]$$

[31]

$$\hat{b} = \sum_{t=2}^{T} Y'_t X'_t \, / \, \sum_{t=2}^{T} (X'_t)^2$$

[32]

$$\text{var}(\hat{a}) = \frac{s^2}{(1-p)^2} \left[\frac{1}{T-1} + \frac{(X'_t)^2}{\sum_t (X'_t)^2} \right]$$

[33]

$$\text{var}(\dot{b}) = s^2 / \sum_t (X'_t)^2 \qquad [34]$$

Moreover, s^2 is computed according to the following formula:

$$s^2 = \frac{\sum_t [Y'_t - \hat{a} - \dot{b}X'_t]^2}{T-3} \qquad [35]$$

where $T-3$ reflects the fact that the number of observations is reduced by employing the transformation. Compare these estimates to those in the previous section.

It has been suggested that the number of observations can be fully restored by employing the following transformation for the first observation:

$$\begin{aligned} \sqrt{1-p^2} \;\; Y_1 &= Y_1 - p\,Y_0 \\ \sqrt{1-p^2} \;\; X_1 &= X_1 - p\,X_0 \end{aligned} \qquad [36]$$

since Y_0 and X_0 are not observable. This transformation will preserve the number of observations, but it must be used with extreme care (Wonnacott and Wonnacott, 1970:142). It is appropriate if and only if the process generating the error has been going on undisturbed for a long time previous to collecting the data. In practice, however, the first observation is taken after a war or some similar catastrophic event, which seriously disturbs the error. In such cases the above transformation should not be used and the first observation must be dropped from the sample.

The above estimates of $\hat{a}$, $\dot{b}$, $\text{var}(\hat{a})$, $\text{var}(\dot{b})$, and s^2 are efficient, and hence we have located an estimation technique with desirable properties for incorporating available information about the relationship among the error terms themselves into the estimation process. What we have done is assumed a specific form of the process generating the autocorrelated residuals (i.e., first order autoregressive), transformed the regression model with autocorrelated errors into one that satisfies all of the assumptions of the simple model, and then applied OLS to the transformed data. Specifically, the transformed variables are constructed in the following way (Hibbs, 1974:269):

$$\begin{aligned} Y'_1 &= \sqrt{1-p^2}\;\; Y_1 & t &= 1 \\ Y'_t &= Y_t - pY_{t-1} & t &= 2, 3, \ldots, T \\ X'_1 &= \sqrt{1-p^2}\;\; X_1 & t &= 1 \\ X'_t &= X_t - pX_{t-1} & t &= 2, 3, \ldots, T \end{aligned} \qquad [37]$$

Y_t' is then directly regressed on X_t', which has the effect of transforming the errors to

$$e_t' = e_t - pe_{t-1} \quad t = 2, 3, \ldots, T$$

Since the e_t are assumed to follow the first order autoregressive pattern, the error of the revised model becomes:

$$e_t' = pe_{t-1} + v_t - pe_{t-1}$$

$$= v_t$$

[38]

Then, because v_t is assumed to meet assumptions 3, 4, and 5, the revised model likewise meets these assumptions.

The approach of transforming the data and applying OLS to the transformed data is usually referred to as *Generalized Least Squares* (hereafter GLS). The direct derivation of the GLS estimates requires more mathematical skills than this monograph assumes, so we will not derive the estimates here. It can be shown, however, that transforming the data and applying OLS yields GLS estimates of a and b. The only qualification is that GLS assumes that we know both the process generating the disturbances and the parameters of that process. In the present case, this involves knowing that the process is a first order autoregressive process and knowing the value of the parameter p. The GLS estimation technique is available only so long as we have the necessary information. If, as is usually the case, we lack the knowledge necessary to undertake GLS, it is possible to determine the nature of the process generating the errors, estimate its parameters (in the case of the first order process, p), and then transform the data and apply OLS. Hibbs (1974:282) calls this procedure *pseudo-GLS*. As we shall see in the following section, pseudo-GLS estimates can often be achieved without the use of special computer programs.

PSEUDO-GLS ESTIMATION

There are an enormous number of different approaches to pseudo-GLS estimation, three of which will be discussed in this section and one in the following section. In principle, each technique estimates p and then transforms the data and uses OLS; the major differences between the methods concerns the estimation of p. It should be noted that the methods differ widely in terms of difficulty, need for specialized computer programs, and cost. After presenting each of the methods, we will examine the results of an experiment in which the small sample properties of each of the techniques are compared.

Hildreth-Lu. The first method estimates all the model parameters simultaneously. Hildreth and Lu (see Kmenta, 1971:282-287) consider the following equation (equation 30):

$$Y_t - pY_{t-1} = a(1-p) + b(X_t - pX_t) + v_t$$

where a, b, p, and σ^2 are not known. Given this equation, Hildreth and Lu offer the following approach:

(1) Assume that p is unknown. In this case the GLS estimates of a and b can be directly computed using equations 31 and 32. These estimates, say â and b̂, can then be used to compute s^2 which would be:

$$s^2 = (1/T-2) \sum_t \ [(Y_t - pY_{t-1}) - â(1-p) - b̂(X_t - pX_t)]^2 \qquad [39]$$

Now different values of p will lead to different values of â, b̂, and s^2.

(2) Search over different values of p, say −.95, −.90, −.85, . . ., .85, .90, .95, and select that p̂ (and the corresponding â and b̂) that leads to the smallest s^2.

The solution will be the equation (with a given value of p) which has the smallest sum of squared residuals. The standard errors of â and b̂ can be computed from the GLS formula (equations 32 and 33) after replacing p by p̂. The Hildreth-Lu estimates can be obtained from the Time-Series Processor (TSP) program by specifying the model and the values of p to be searched. Note that the more values of p that we include to be searched, the more expensive the program run will be. As a consequence, if we suspect positive serial correlation, there would be no reason to search negative values of p. While this procedure is quite complicated in theory, it is in practice very simple to implement.

Cochrane-Orcutt. A second alternative is the Cochrane-Orcutt method, which again requires a special program. The method, as described by Kmenta (1971:288), consists of the following steps:

(1) Obtain OLS estimates of

$$Y_t = a + bX_t + e_t \qquad [40]$$

and calculate the estimated residuals $ê_1, ê_2, . . ., ê_1$. Use these to obtain a "first round" estimate of p, say p̂, which is defined as

$$p̂ = \Sigma ê_t ê_{t-1} / \Sigma ê_{t-1}^2 \qquad t = 2, 3, . . ., T \qquad [41]$$

(2) Construct Y'_t and X'_t and obtain OLS estimates of

$$Y'_t = a' + bX'_t + v_t \qquad\qquad [42]$$

These second round estimates are called $\hat{a}$ and $\hat{b}$ and lead to second round residuals, $\hat{e}_1, \hat{e}_2, \ldots, \hat{e}_T$ (where $\hat{e}_t = Y_t - \hat{a} - \hat{b}X_t$). These are then used to obtain a new estimate of p, say $\hat{\hat{p}}$,

$$\hat{\hat{p}} = \Sigma\hat{e}_t\hat{e}_{t-1} / \Sigma\hat{e}^2_{t-1} \qquad t = 2, 3, \ldots, T \qquad\qquad [43]$$

(3) Construct new variables Y'_t and X'_t using $\hat{\hat{p}}$ instead of $\hat{p}$ and then proceed as in step 2.

This procedure should be continued until the values of the estimators converge, i.e., until we obtain the same values for the parameters round after round. Cochrane and Orcutt have shown that the procedure does converge, and that the final round estimates are identical to those obtained by the Hildreth-Lu technique for large samples.

The Cochrane-Orcutt procedure can be reduced to two stages by stopping after obtaining the second round estimates, $\hat{a}$ and $\hat{b}$. These estimators have the same large sample properties as the more extended procedure and, furthermore, have the virtue of being computable using the Statistical Package for the Social Sciences (SPSS). The $\hat{e}_t$ can be computed using $Y_t - \hat{a} - \hat{b}X_t$ and a COMPUTE statement, and $\hat{e}_{t-1}$ can be computed similarly. The estimates of the standard errors of a and b can be obtained by using equations 32 and 33 and replacing p by $\hat{p}$.

First Differences. Perhaps the most widely used and/or suggested procedure for dealing with autocorrelation is first differences. That is, we assume that p = 1, transform the original data into first differences ($Y_t - Y_{t-1}$ and $X_t - X_{t-1}$), and then estimate the following equation with OLS:

$$Y_t - Y_{t-1} = a^* + b(X_t - X_{t-1}) + (e_t - e_{t-1}) \qquad\qquad [44]$$

Note that since

$$Y_t = a + bX_t + e_t$$

$$Y_{t-1} = a + bX_{t-1} + e_{t-1}$$

it follows that $a^* = 0$ and $v_t = e_t - e_{t-1}$. The rationale of this method is the belief that the true value of p is close to 1.0. Furthermore, we do not expect to obtain an estimate of a. Kmenta (1971:290-292) shows in great detail why the use of first differences is not recommended unless it is really believed that p is close to 1.0. Otherwise the procedure may lead to some rather erroneous inferences. The advantage of the first difference technique is that it involves no separate estimation of p.

SMALL SAMPLE PROPERTIES

It has been shown that, at least in principle, these various multi-stage procedures are more efficient than simple OLS (Johnston, 1972:264). This leaves two additional questions unanswered: (1) does the gain in efficiency actually show up in small samples, and (2) is there any variation in the small sample efficiency of the various estimators? The small sample properties of the alternative estimators of the regression coefficients in models with autoregressive disturbances are generally unknown, because the determination of the sampling distributions of these estimators is very complicated. We can get some idea about the small sample behavior of these estimators by deriving their sampling distribution experimentally. This can be done only for specific models and specific populations of the disturbances. Sampling experiments of this sort (Kmenta, 1971; Griliches and Rao, 1969) are known as "Monte Carlo experiments" because of their similarity to games of chance.

To provide some practical guidelines for the consumer of various pseudo-GLS techniques, let us examine the results of the Kmenta experiment (1971: 292-295) in which he compares OLS with the Hildreth-Lu and two step Cochrane-Orcutt techniques. The results have been recorded in Table 2, and show that all of the estimators are unbiased and that the OLS estimates are inefficient relative to the others. The Hildreth-Lu and two step Cochrane-Orcutt procedures are nearly identical for the samples of 20 and larger. In the smallest sample the Hildreth-Lu technique does appear to be efficient. Experimental results are difficult to generalize from, but they do give some indication that the small sample behavior of the individual estimators may be similar to the previously discussed large sample properties.

TABLE 2
Monte Carlo Results
$$(Y = 10 + 2X_t + e_t)$$

	Estimator					
Sample Size	Ordinary Least Squares		Hildreth-Lu		Cochrane-Orcutt (2-stage)	
	mean	SD	mean	SD	mean	SD
10	2.0070	.1029	2.0079	.0634	2.0058	.0754
20	2.0008	.0634	1.9995	.0402	1.9997	.0412
100	2.0001	.0201	1.9990	.0136	1.999	.0136

Source: Kmenta (1971, p. 293).

EXTENSION TO MULTIPLE REGRESSION

To this point we have concentrated on the bivariate version of time series regression model. The reader may be wondering what will happen if we extend the model to one with k regressors and autocorrelation, i.e.,

$$Y_t = a + b_1 X_{1t} + b_2 X_{2t} + \ldots + b_k X_{kt} + e_t$$

$$e_t = p e_{t-1} + v_t$$

[45]

If we maintain all of the basic assumptions and add two more (no multi-collinearity and that we have fewer regressors than observations), then the extension of the previous techniques to the multiple regression case is straight-forward.

The estimating formula changes to reflect the inclusion of additional explanatory variables (Kmenta, 1971:347-357), and the residual is estimated as

$$\hat{e}_t = Y_t - \hat{a} - \hat{b}_1 X_{1t} - \hat{b}_2 X_{2t} - \ldots - \hat{b}_k X_{kt}$$

The consequences of violation of the nonautoregression assumption are identical and the tests are applicable. Note, however, that the Durbin-Watson test requires that we use the number of regressors k + 1 (the 1 refers to the constant term) to determine the appropriate upper and lower limits. In terms of pseudo-GLS estimation, we would proceed to estimate equation 45 with OLS to obtain e_t. Using e_t we can employ one of the previously mentioned algorithms to estimate p, and then transform the data as follows (Hibbs, 1974):

$$Y_1' = \sqrt{1 - p^2}\ Y_1 \quad t = 1$$

$$X_{k1}' = \sqrt{1 - p^2}\ X_{k1} \quad t = 1;\ k = 1, 2, \ldots, K$$

[46]

$$Y_t' = Y_t - p Y_{t-1} \quad \text{for } t = 2, 3, \ldots, T$$

$$X_{kt}' = X_{kt} - p X_{kt-1} \quad \text{for } t = 2, 3, \ldots, T;\ k = 1, 2, \ldots, K$$

The GLS estimates are then obtained by regressing Y_t' on the X_{kt}'.

THE RATIO GOAL HYPOTHESIS RECONSIDERED

Equation 1 presented a model in which U.S. and USSR defense expenditures are related to one another. The parameter estimates and related statistics were presented earlier. The Durbin-Watson test indicates that there is significant serial correlation in the estimated residuals, however, which leads us to conclude that, since the autoregression is positive, the fit of the model is exaggerated. In order to overcome this problem we will use one of the pseudo-GLS techniques discussed in the previous section.

In order to provide an additional comparison, each of the three techniques suggested in the previous section has been used to re-estimate equation 1. The results of this re-estimation are displayed in Table 3, which shows that these three pseudo-GLS techniques yield very similar results. All have a reasonably small, positive constant term and a slope of approximately .75. The most remarkable fact is the degree to which the magnitude of the fit has been reduced: the R^2's drop from .82 to approximately .30. This is certainly a consequence of the fact that $\hat{p}$ is so high. Given $\hat{p}$'s of .9 or higher, the OLS technique drastically underestimates the true variance (see equation 21). Had we simply chosen to ignore the serial correlation, we would have been led to make exaggerated claims for the explanatory power of the simple ratio goal model. Based on the pseudo-GLS estimates, the explanatory power of this version of the ratio goal model is not very great.

It should be noted that there is some problem with the computation of the R^2 statistic for the GLS regression model. A discussion of the problems with commonly used GLS goodness of fit measures is provided by Buse (1973). The derivation of the appropriate goodness of fit statistics requires some manipulation of the statistics usually reported. The computation of these statistics will be discussed in a later section.

One important feature of the pseudo-GLS estimates which merits some attention is the post-GLS Durbin-Watson d's. As can be seen, all are higher than the upper bound of 1.07 for the .01 level, but all are lower than the upper bound of 1.34 for the .05 level. Depending upon the significance level we chose, they are low enough to suggest that there is some serial correlation remaining in the model. There are at least two possibilities at this point. First, it could be that we have misspecified the process generating the disturbances. That is, the process generating the disturbances may be something other than a first order autoregressive process. A range of possible alternatives to the first order autoregressive model will be presented in the final section of the monograph.

TABLE 3
Alternative GLS Estimates for Equation 1

Technique	a(1-p)	b	R^2	s.e.	D.W.	$\hat{p}$
Hildreth-Lu	3222	.811	.33	4851	1.17	.90
Cochrane-Orcutt	2594	.701	.27	4800	1.22	.95
First Differences	964	.771	.22	4912	1.18	1.00

Second, the equation itself could be misspecified. On the one hand, some relevant variable(s) may have been ommitted from the equation (Kmenta, 1971:297). On the other hand, the form of the equation could be misspecified. If, for example, there is a curvilinear relationship between the two variables and we estimated equation 1, the pattern of residuals would suggest positive autocorrelation. Thus the residuals can indicate autocorrelation when the equation is actually nonlinear. Kmenta (1971:451-472) introduces a variety of nonlinear models which he divides into two groups—intrinsically linear and intrinsically nonlinear. The former (e.g., polynomial regression) can be estimated with OLS (or GLS), whereas the latter require special estimation algorithms. A discussion of nonlinear models is beyond the scope of the present inquiry. Suffice it to say that autocorrelation can indicate specification error.

3. TIME SERIES REGRESSION ANALYSIS: LAGGED CASE

To the reader who has little previous experience with time series regression analysis, the fact that we may have to go to a great deal of trouble to obtain unbiased estimators of the coefficient variances even though the coefficient estimates themselves are unbiased may be somewhat distressing. The preceding discussion nevertheless provides a base upon which to assess models of different types; in many cases these different models face much more severe problems of estimation. The class of models that we will focus on in this section are those that incorporate lagged endogenous and exogenous variables.

To this point we have examined only models which posit a contemporaneous relationship between the left and right hand sides of an equation, that is, the observations on both sets of variables are taken during the same time period. Depending upon the substantive relationship we are modeling, it may be plausible to incorporate time lags into the basic model. There are essentially two types of time lags: (1) lagged values of the exogenous variables and (2) lagged values of the endogenous variable. As we shall see, the former create very few new estimation problems, whereas the latter introduce a range of new problems. Each of these models will be discussed in turn.

LAGGED EXOGENOUS VARIABLES

Modeling some relationships often requires the inclusion of lagged exogenous variables. For example, we might argue that it is plausible to explicitly incorporate time lags into a relationship because the dependent variable cannot be expected to respond immediately to a specific increase or decrease in the independent variables. A lag formulation acknowledges that it takes time for one variable to affect another. One possible formulation is to assume that it takes a specific period of time, say one year, for USSR spending to effect U.S. spending. In this case we would estimate the following model:

$$Y_t = a + bX_{t-1} + e_t \qquad [47]$$

where the terms have been defined earlier. If the relevant assumptions are satisfied, the discussion of the previous section is applicable, and we can estimate the equation, test for autocorrelation, and then take appropriate corrective action if there is any indication of significant autocorrelation.

The only possible problem with this model is that it is usually not possible to specify the exact amount of time that it takes X_t to affect Y_t. If there is no compelling reason for assuming a given response time, we may wish to allow it to be spread over several successive time periods instead. For example, suppose that the effect of Soviet spending is spread over n time periods with a partial effect relating to each lagged period:

$$Y_t = a + b_0 X_t + b_1 X_{t-1} = \ldots + b_n X_{t-n} + e_t \qquad [48]$$

This specification is usually referred to as a *distributed lag model*. Under the usual assumptions of the multiple regression model there are no new estimation problems, at least in principle. OLS or GLS can be used to generate unbiased, relatively efficient, and consistent estimates. Practical problems posed by the distributed lag model usually preclude the direct application of OLS and GLS, however. One problem is that the lagged values of the explanatory variables are likely to be highly correlated with each other, thus creating potential problems with multicollinearity. This makes it difficult to separate the effects of the various independent variables on the dependent variable (Kelejian and Oates, 1974:147). A second problem is that the long lag may leave very few degrees of freedom. If n is large, there will be a large number of parameters to estimate. Finally, for every lagged variable we enter in a relationship, an observation must be omitted. The fact that the data set used in the example has only 16 observations drastically limits the length of lag we can investigate. Whether or not this is a problem generally depends upon the sample size, however.

To deal with these problems, some restrictions are usually imposed on the lag weights (i.e., b_0, b_1, ..., b_n). This reduces the number of observations lost due to the lagging and/or the number of parameters to be estimated. For example, we may impose the restrictions that the weights must be positive and decline over time. Another possibility is that the weights are all positive and will rise and thereafter decline. It may also be that the weights can be approximated by a polynomial of degree q which is less than n. (A discussion of the individual techniques involved is a bit too advanced for this monograph, but the interested reader may consult any standard econometrics book under topics of geometric, Pascal, or Almon lags. For an example of the use of the Almon technique in political science, see Ostrom and Hoole, forthcoming.)

Thus far, we have discussed the estimation of lagged relationships where only lagged exogenous variables are considered. The basic approaches to this task are (1) direct estimation with OLS or GLS, or (2) specification that the weights follow some pattern and estimate accordingly. In each case, care must be given to the problem of autocorrelation in order to ensure that the variance estimates are not biased. These methods work, however, only as long as there are no lagged endogenous variables in the equation. The introduction of lagged endogenous variables creates a number of new considerations.

LAGGED ENDOGENOUS VARIABLES

Continuing with the defense expenditure example that has been developed throughout this paper, the previous level at which the U.S. has been spending may be the principal determinant of current spending. That is,

$$Y_t = a + bY_{t-1} + e_t \tag{49}$$

The substantive justification for such a hypothesis has been offered by Rattinger (1975:575), who feels that "bureaucratic momentum" exists whereby "the budget administered by a government bureaucracy in any given year is expected to amount to an approximately fixed percentage higher than the one the previous year." Such a relationship is formally represented in equation 49.

To estimate this model, OLS is applied to equation 49. The results are as follows:

$$Y_t = -3614 + 1.12\,Y_{t-1}$$
$$\quad\;\; (0.60) \quad (9.02)$$
$$R^2 = .85 \quad \text{s.e.} = \$5.40 \text{ billion} \quad \text{D.W.} = 1.18$$

As can be seen, this model provides an extraordinarily good fit to the expenditure data; it also suggests that the U.S. increases its level of spending by approximately 12% per year.

We might ask if there is any problem with serial correlation in the "bureaucratic momentum" model. A check of the Durbin-Watson d-statistic indicates that there is some question as to whether serial correlation is a problem. Therefore, we might be led to conclude that the bureaucratic momentum model is quite accurate. This is not the case, however—not only is there a problem with the estimated model, but with the use of the Durbin-Watson d as well. It is to a discussion of these issues that we now turn.

For a discussion of the basic autoregressive model, we will focus on the following model (Johnston, 1972:303-313):

$$y_t = b y_{t-1} + e_t \qquad [50]$$

where y_t and y_{t-1} are expressed as mean deviates (i.e., $y_t = Y_t - \overline{Y}$). In later sections we will extend the discussion to situations in which there are further lagged values of y_t and additional explanatory variables. The estimation procedures and problems depend upon the assumptions made about the e_t. The subsequent discussion distinguishes between the following two sets of assumptions:

A. e_t meets assumptions 3, 4, and 5

B. $e_t = p e_{t-1} + v_t$

    v_t meets assumptions 3, 4, and 5

    $-1 < p < +1$

Assumption A posits that the e_t's have a zero mean, constant variance, and zero covariance. This is the simplest assumption, and so long as $b < 1$, the only complication is that y_{t-1} appears on the right hand side of equation 50. Assumption B indicates that the e_t's follow a first order autoregressive process, which means that they are no longer random.

Assumption A

First of all, it must be re-emphasized that we are assuming that the errors are not autocorrelated, so that the only complication arises because of the lagged y being used as an explanatory variable (Johnston, 1972:305). If one applied OLS directly to equation 50, the estimate of b, say b*, is as follows:

$$b^* = \frac{\sum_t y_t y_{t-1}}{\sum_t y_{t-1}^2} \qquad [51]$$

Malinvaud (1970:551) shows that under certain very restrictive assumptions (i.e., $b < 1$, y_0 is random, b is small in absolute value, and T is large) the expected value of b* is

$$E[b^*] = b \left[1 - \frac{2}{T} \right] \qquad [52]$$

Thus as T becomes large, the bias (defined as $-2b/T$) tends to be very small. Malinvaud points out, however, that for samples of approximately 20 the bias reaches about 10 percent of the true value. Thus, the simple autoregressive model yields biased though consistent and relatively efficient estimates of the coefficient of the lagged dependent variable so long as the errors are not serially correlated.

Malinvaud (1970:552), after reporting upon the results of various other models, concludes:

> these results confirm that the theory developed for regression models is not applicable as is to autoregressive models. But they suggest that in practice no serious error is committed if we apply the usual methods conceived for regression models to the treatment of autoregressive models. *Of course this optimistic conclusion is valid only in so far as the errors e_t are not autocorrelated.* (Emphasis added.)

Thus, if the model in equation 50 does not suffer from autocorrelated error terms, b^* is biased but consistent. The decision as to whether or not the errors are serially correlated is not as straightforward as in the nonlagged case—specifically, the usual Durbin-Watson test is no longer appropriate. As a result, we will examine the properties of the estimators under Assumption B and then present an alternative test for autocorrelated errors.

Assumption B

The combination of lagged y values and autocorrelated disturbances means that the OLS estimates will not be consistent. As Johnston (1972:307) notes:

> Autocorrelated disturbances without lagged Y values do not produce biased estimators, even in small samples; lagged Y values with random disturbance terms will give OLS estimators which are consistent, though biased in finite samples; the combination of the two problems, however, throws OLS off-beam and gives inconsistent estimators.

The primary reason for this is that the explanatory variable, y_{t-1}, is no longer uncorrelated with the current disturbance, e_t; i.e., $E(y_{t-1}e_t) \neq 0$. This occurs because y_t directly depends on e_t, y_{t-1} on e_{t-1}, and so on. Therefore, since e_t and e_{t-1} are directly related (by Assumption B), y_{t-1} is related to e_t. To see this, lag equation 50 by one period, multiply by e_t, and take expected values:

$$E[y_{t-1}e_t] = b\,E[y_{t-2}e_t] + E[e_te_{t-1}]$$

$$= 0 - p\sigma^2 \qquad\qquad [53]$$

$$= -p\sigma^2$$

We have shown that the covariance between e_t and y_{t-1} is nonzero under the first order autoregressive assumption. Thus autocorrelation in the presence of lagged dependent variables means that the explanatory variable will be correlated with the current disturbance. This is a direct violation of assumption 2 and means that the parameter estimates will be inconsistent (Kelejian and Oates, 1974:261).

In order to ascertain the consequences of the inconsistency for the parameter estimates, consider the following development of Hibbs (1974:296). If we lag equation 50 by one period and multiply through by p we get:

$$py_{t-1} = pby_{t-2} + pe_{t-1} \qquad [54]$$

which when solved for pe_{t-1} yields:

$$pe_{t-1} = py_{t-1} - pby_{t-2} \qquad [55]$$

Hence the original equation can be written

$$
\begin{aligned}
y_t &= by_{t-1} + pe_{t-1} + v_t \\
&= by_{t-1} + py_{t-1} - pby_{t-2} + v_t \qquad [56] \\
&= (b+p)y_{t-1} - bpy_{t-2} + v_t
\end{aligned}
$$

Thus, if we go ahead and apply OLS to equation 50 when Assumption B is in force, this leads to the classic problem of omitted variables (see Uslaner 1978), in which the coefficient estimate of y_{t-1} picks up some of the influence of the excluded variable y_{t-2}. The type of problems that this leads to can be seen from the following argument. In the present case, the true coefficient of y_{t-1} is $b+p$, and $-pb$ is the true coefficient of the omitted variable, y_{t-2}. The OLS estimate of b (b*) in the original model is given in equation 51; it has as its expected value (assuming autocorrelated errors)

$$E[b^*] = b + \left[p - \frac{pb \sum_t y_t y_{t-1}}{\sum_t y_{t-1}^2} \right] \qquad [57]$$

It can be shown, furthermore, that this bias will not disappear as the sample size becomes infinitely large. The asymptotic bias, which is the bias in the estimator as the sample size becomes very large, is given by

$$p(1 - b^2) / (1 + pb) \qquad [58]$$

Therefore we are likely to overestimate the impact of y_{t-1} whenever p is positive (Hibbs, 1974:292). In other words, the influence of y_{t-1} in auto-regressive equations is usually exaggerated.

Hibbs shows that the parameter estimates are inconsistent and asymptotically biased so that no matter how large a sample one possesses, the estimates will not converge to the true values. Table 4 indicates the magnitude of the bias in b^* for various values of b and p. The principal result of Table 4 is that, for small values of b and large values of p, the bias is extremely large (remember that b^* is constrained between zero and one).

In addition to the bias and inconsistency of b^* when OLS is applied to a model with autocorrelated errors and a lagged dependent variable, the OLS residuals $\hat{e}_t$ no longer provide an accurate reflection of the true underlying disturbances, because the lagged values of y_t tend to absorb the systematic impact of the disturbances. In short, the previously outlined procedures for estimating p and d are now seriously biased. For example, suppose we use b^* to estimate the residuals, i.e.,

$$\hat{e}_t = y_t - b^* y_{t-1} \qquad [59]$$

and the $\hat{e}_t$'s to estimate the first order autoregressive coefficient, p, i.e.,

$$\hat{p} = \sum_t \hat{e}_t \hat{e}_{t-1} / \sum_t \hat{e}_{t-1}^2 \qquad [60]$$

Malinvaud (1970:460-461) has shown that the asymptotic bias of $\hat{p}$ is

$$-p(1 - b^2) / (1 + pb) \qquad [61]$$

which is the *exact negative* of the asymptotic bias in b^*. Thus if p is positive the bias will be negative—and if b is small and p is large and positive, we will tend to seriously underestimate the true magnitude of the serial correlation.

TABLE 4
Values of Asymptotic Bias of
b^* for Various Values of b and p

b	.2	.2	.2	.5	.5	.5	.8	.8	.8
p	.1	.5	.8	.1	.5	.8	.1	.5	.8
Asym. Bias	.09	.44	.66	.07	.30	.43	.03	.13	.18

Source: Johnston (1972, p. 308).

Turning now to the Durbin-Watson d-statistic, Johnston (1972:310) has shown that its asymptotic bias is

$$2p(1 - b^2) / (1 + pb) \qquad [62]$$

which is *exactly twice* the bias of b. Thus if p is positive, the bias in d is upward; the seriousness of this is clear if one notes that small values of d are associated with positive serial correlation. Table 5 shows the bias in d for various values of b when p = .5 and d = 1.00. The bias is positive in all cases and usually quite large. The conclusion that we can draw from this is that d is biased toward 2.00 (the value for random disturbances) when there is positive serial correlation and the model contains a lagged endogenous variable.

What can we make of these results? Perhaps most importantly, if we have a model with lagged values of the dependent variable serving as explanatory variables and the positive serial correlation, we are likely to be overconfident about the fit of the model. That is, we are likely to overestimate b, underestimate p, and d will be biased toward 2.00. This is a very dangerous situation because we will be led into making strong inferences about the model when in fact there are serious problems. Johnston (1972:311) indicates that these conclusions are excessively alarmist, because it is only in the case of the simple model used in this section that one obtains such results. In fact, Malinvaud (1970:462-465) shows that, in the presence of additional explanatory variables (x_t and x_{t-1}), the bias is reduced in absolute value even though it is still significantly large. Thus we are likely to overestimate the coefficient of y_{t-1} at the expense of the x_t's—which, in turn, means that we may make erroneous inferences regarding the importance of the dynamic terms. It is therefore important to develop bcth a new indicator of serial correlation and estimation methods which can be used in the presence of significant serial correlation.

TESTING FOR AUTOCORRELATION IN MODELS WITH LAGGED ENDOGENOUS VARIABLES

Given the results of the previous section, it is necessary to develop an alternative to the conventional Durbin-Watson test for serial correlation when we have a model in which one or more explanatory variables are lagged endogenous variables. Durbin (1970) presents two such tests.

TABLE 5
Values of Asymptotic Bias in d When p = .50 and d = 1.0

b	.9	.7	.5	.3	−.5	−.7	−.9
Asym. bias	.13	.38	.60	.79	1.00	.78	.35

Source: Johnston (1972, p. 311).

The first test is called Durbin's h, and even though it is not widely used or discussed, it can be easily computed from any standard OLS regression package. The test consists of the following steps (Johnston, 1972:312-313):

(1) Generate OLS estimates of the parameters

(2) Estimate p. Johnston (1972) suggests using the following procedure: $\hat{p} = 1 - d/2$, where d is the Durbin-Watson d.

(3) Determine $var(b^*)$, where $var(b^*)$ is the sampling variance of b^*, the coefficient of Y_{t-1}. No matter how many lagged values of Y_t are included in an equation, one must still use the variance of the coefficient of Y_{t-1}.

(4) Compute Durbin's h using the following formula:

$$h = \hat{p} \sqrt{\frac{T}{1 - Tvar(b^*)}}$$

where T is the sample size.

Durbin's h is then tested as a *standard nomal variable*. (Note: *do not* use Durbin-Watson tables.) That is, if $h > 1.64$, we would reject the hypothesis of zero autocorrelation at the .05 level (Johnston 1972:313). This test is primarily for samples greater than 30; there is no evidence for its behavior in smaller samples.

The second test is likewise developed by Durbin, and is used if $Tvar(b^*) > 1$. In such cases Durbin's h breaks down, because it involves the square root of a negative number. As a second possibility Durbin suggests this procedure:

(1) Estimate the relationship with OLS

(2) Compute $\hat{e}_t$ and $\hat{e}_{t-1}$

(3) Regress e_t on Y_{t-1}, X_t, X_{t-1}, and e_{t-1}—in short, on all variables on the right hand side of the original equation *plus* $\hat{e}_{t-1}$.

(4) Test the significance of the coefficient of e_{t-1} in the regression in step 3.

This test is conducted using the standard t-test; if it is significant at the chosen level, there is an indication of significant autocorrelation.

There have been suggestions that distribution-free tests, such as the Geary test, are appropriate in models with lagged values of the dependent variables. However, one of the above two tests should be used instead, since the use of distribution-free tests in such models has not been thoroughly investigated.

Turning to the results for equation 49, it is now possible to conduct a proper test for serial correlation. Since $T = 16$, $var(b_1^*) = .05$, and $\hat{p} = .41$,

Durbin's h is 3.66. Thus we can reject the null hypothesis of zero serial correlation of the .01 level.

ESTIMATION

In the discussion of models which do not include a lagged endogenous variable but do have autocorrelated errors, an estimation technique called Generalized Least Squares (GLS) was presented. All of that discussion is applicable to models with lagged endogenous variables. Consider the following model:

$$Y_t = a + b_1 Y_{t-1} + b_2 X_t + e_t$$

$$e_t = p e_{t-1} + v_t \qquad [63]$$

$$v_t \text{ meets assumptions } 3, 4, \text{ and } 5$$

Then, if p is known, all one need do is transform the equation as follows:

$$Y_t - p Y_{t-1} = a(1-p) + b_1(Y_{t-1} - p Y_{t-2}) + b_2(X_t - p X_{t-1}) + v_t \qquad [64]$$

and estimate directly with OLS. The estimates which result will be biased, but they will be consistent and asymptotically efficient. This approach is available only so long as p is known. If p is not known, we must determine the nature of the process generating the disturbances, estimate the parameters, and then transform the data—in short, a pseudo-GLS procedure must be used. Unlike the previous discussion, here the presence of lagged values of Y_t means that the usual methods for estimating p will yield inconsistent estimates. Hence the pseudo-GLS procedures to be discussed in this section differ markedly from those in the previous section.

PSEUDO-GLS ESTIMATION

Of the possible approaches to estimating models (such as those presented in the previous section), we will discuss only one. It entails two steps. First, it is necessary to introduce the instrumental variables technique which produces consistent but relatively inefficient estimates. Second, a variation of pseudo-GLS which produces consistent *and* efficient estimates of the model parameters will be presented.

Instrumental Variables

There are essentially two problems with equation 63: first, Y_{t-1} is correlated with the contemporaneous disturbance term, and second, e_t is autocorrelated. The instrumental variables technique deals with the first problem, and hence yields consistent estimates of the regression parameters. The basic problem is that Y_{t-1} is correlated with e_t. The method of instrumental variables (IV) is available whenever we can find a new variable Z_t that is both uncorrelated with the disturbance term and correlated with Y_{t-1}. Kmenta (1971:480) suggests that the following instrument be used:

$$Z_t = X_{t-1} \qquad [65]$$

Clearly, X_{t-1} is not correlated with the disturbance term and is likely to be correlated with Y_{t-1}. Another suggestion (Johnston, 1972:318) is to regress Y_t on lagged values of X_t, using OLS in order to obtain the predicted value, Y_t^*

$$\hat{Y}_t = c_0 + c_1 X_{t-1} + c_2 X_{t-2} + \ldots \qquad [66]$$

The number of lagged X_t values can be decided upon in relation to the number of observations and to incremental explanatory power. The above relation is then lagged by one period to give Y_{t-1}^*; Y_{t-1}^* is, in turn, inserted in place of Y_{t-1}, and OLS can then be applied to the equation to estimate the parameters.

The instrumental variables procedure will yield consistent estimates of the parameters because both explanatory variables are now uncorrelated with the disturbance. The estimates remain inefficient, however, since the residuals are autocorrelated. In short, we are in the situation similar to that of autocorrelation in static models—the estimates are consistent but relatively inefficient because we have not taken the serial correlation into account.

Hibbs (1974) indicates that the standard regression program will not yield appropriate estimates of R^2, σ^2, and so on, when an instrumental variable technique is used. In order to obtain the proper estimates, we must take "the consistent parameter estimates in conjunction with the original data and model to generate goodness of fit statistics" (Hibbs, 1974:297). This involves the following steps:

(1) Regress Y_t on X_{t-1}, X_{t-2}, and so on

(2) Compute Y_{t-1}^* (i.e., $Y_{t-1}^* = \hat{c}_1 X_{t-1} + \hat{c}_2 X_{t-2} \ldots$)

(3) Estimate the following relationship:

$$Y_t = a + b_1 Y_{t-1}^* + b_2 X_t + e_t$$

(4) Use $\hat{a}$, $\hat{b}_1$, $\hat{b}_2$ in the following manner to obtain the goodness of fit statistics:

$$\dot{Y}_t = \hat{a} + \hat{b}_1 Y_{t-1} + \hat{b}_2 X_t$$

which can then be substituted for Y_t into the following

$$R^2 = \frac{\Sigma(Y_t - \dot{Y}_t)^2}{\Sigma(Y_t - \bar{Y})^2}$$

$$S^2 = \frac{\Sigma[(Y_t - \bar{Y}) - \hat{b}_1(Y_{t-1} - \bar{Y}_{t-1}) - \hat{b}_2(X_t - \bar{X})]^2}{T - 3}$$

In order to obtain efficient estimates of the model parameters, it is necessary to take the autocorrelated disturbances into account.

IV-Pseudo GLS

To improve upon the former estimates, the IV technique can be extended as follows (Johnston, 1972:319-320):

(1) Compute the estimated residuals in conjunction with original data and consistently estimated parameters, i.e.,

$$\hat{e}_t = Y_t - \dot{Y}_t$$

(2) Estimate p

$$\hat{p} = \frac{\Sigma \hat{e}_t \hat{e}_{t-1}/T-1}{\Sigma \hat{e}_t^2/T} + \frac{k}{T}$$

where k is the number of parameters in the model.

(3) Use $\hat{p}$ to transform the data in the equation, and apply OLS to the transformed data

$$(Y_t - \hat{p}Y_{t-1}) = a(1-\hat{p}) + b_1(Y_{t-1} - \hat{p}Y_{t-2}) + b_2(X_t - \hat{p}X_{t-1}) + v_t$$

where the actual values of Y_{t-1} and Y_{t-2} are used.

Hibbs (1974:298) observes that the existing experimental evidence suggests that the IV-GLS method outperforms OLS and IV alone—for models such as the one discussed here—when the disturbances are generated by a first order autoregressive process. In addition, there are a number of other techniques which are appropriate for estimating models which have lagged endogenous variables. For example, there are several maximum likelihood search techniques available, but they are conceptually complex and computationally expensive (Hibbs, 1977). Although they may perform better than the IV-GLS technique they require special programs, whereas the IV-GLS estimates can be derived with a standard regression program (in several steps).

A REVISED RATIO GOAL MODEL

Earlier in this section we saw that equation 49 gives some indication of significant serial correlation. The tentative conclusion we must draw is that the model, as estimated, is invalid. In order to estimate the model correctly, it would be necessary to employ the IV-GLS technique described in the last section. But since we have no explanatory variables to use as instrumental variables, it is not possible to apply this technique to equation 49. Consequently we face a problem which can be solved only by offering an instrumental variable, which in turn necessitates reformulating the model.

All is not loss, however, since there is considerable substantive literature which argues that the simple ratio goal and bureaucratic momentum models ought to be combined into a single model with the following form:

$$Y_t = a + b_1 Y_{t-1} + b_2 X_t + e_t \qquad [67]$$

where all of the symbols have been identified previously.

As a first step, OLS has been applied to equation 67. The results are summarized under step 1 in Table 6. The equation seems to be relatively well supported, because it accounts for 89 percent of the variance with a small standard error. There is a definite problem with serial correlation, however, indicated by a Durbin's h of 4.29. Because there is significant serial correlation, we know that the parameter estimates are inconsistent and that our inferences are likely to be erroneous. The effects of the serial correlation must therefore be removed.

To overcome this problem, the multi-staged IV-pseudo GLS estimation technique has been employed. The results from the various steps are displayed in Table 6. Step 2 is the estimation of the predicted value for the lagged endogenous variable, Y_{t-1}^*. In step 3, this value is substituted into equation 67 for Y_{t-1} and the parameters are estimated with OLS. In step 4, the resulting parameters are used in conjunction with the original data to provide an indication of the fit of the model. Even though the parameter estimates are consistent, there is still a problem created by the presence of serial correlation in the estimated residuals.

From our discussion in the second section, we know that serial correlation creates problems with respect to the inferences we can make. Therefore, in step 5 the residuals (i.e., $Y_t - \hat{Y}_t$) from step 4 are used to compute $\hat{p}$ in the manner previously outlined. The result is that $\hat{p} = .68$. This value is used to transform the original data, and in step 6 the original equation is reestimated. As a result of the six steps of the IV-pseudo GLS procedure, the parameters of equation 67 have been appropriately estimated.

Having obtained consistent and efficient estimates of the parameters, attention can be given to the substantive interpretation of the revised ratio goal

TABLE 6
Estimates from the Six Steps Required to Obtain
IV-GLS Estimates for Equation 67

Step 1

$$Y_t = -9726 + .686\ Y_{t-1} + .742\ X_t$$
$$\quad\ \ (1.63)\quad (3.08)\qquad\ (2.22)$$

$$R^2 = .89 \qquad h = 4.29$$

Step 2

$$Y^*_{t-1} = -4247 + .807\ X_{t-1} + .660\ X_{t-2}$$
$$\qquad\quad\ (0.53)\quad (1.52)\qquad\ (1.23)$$

$$R^2 = .78 \qquad D.W. = .89$$

Step 3

$$Y_t = -9426 + .228\ Y^*_{t-1} + 1.340\ X_t$$
$$\quad\ \ (1.20)\quad (0.25)\qquad\ \ (1.13)$$

$$R^2 = .82 \qquad D.W. = .82$$

Step 4

$$\hat{Y}_t = -9426 + .228\ Y_{t-1} + 1.340\ X_t$$

$$R^2 = .86$$

Step 5

$$\hat{p} = .67$$

Step 6

$$(Y_t - .67\ Y_{t-1}) = 663 + .545(Y_{t-1} - 67Y_{t-2}) + .636(X_t - .67\ X_{t-1})$$
$$\qquad\qquad\qquad\quad\ (0.18)\ (2.59)\qquad\qquad\qquad (1.72)$$

$$R^2 = .70 \qquad D.W. = 1.49$$

model. The first thing to notice is that the overall fit of the model has been lowered, since the R^2 drops from .89 to .70 and the individual t-ratios are likewise reduced. In addition, using the usual serial correlation indicators, there is no evidence of significant serial correlation in the estimated residuals. Despite these reductions, the revised ratio goal model appears to be supported by the data: it provides a reasonable approximation of the U.S. defense expenditure policymaking process.

4. FORECASTING

To this point we have concentrated on establishing relationships between variables over time: within the confines of a given sample we have been interested in ascertaining the nature and strength of the relationship between the dependent and the independent variables. Having accomplished this, it is now reasonable to consider the uses to which we can put an estimated model. One of the primary uses of time series regression models is to generate forecasts of the dependent variable. The principal goal in the forecasting context is to extrapolate beyond the confines of the sample and thereby make generalizations to non-sample situations (Klein, 1971:10). Therefore, throughout the remainder of this paper, a forecast (or prediction) is defined as "the attempt to make scientific statements about non-sample situations on the basis of relationships determined from sample observations" (Klein, 1971:10).

Forecasts of this type have at least two distinct uses. First, they can be used to evaluate a model whose parameters have been estimated. In order to convince potential consumers that a model is worthwhile as a forecasting device, it is usually necessary to provide some evidence that the model in question is capable of generating accurate forecasts. Second, a series of forecasts can be used to make inferences concerning the policy implications of certain types of behavior. Once a model has been validated for use in forecasting, one can make forecasts conditional on certain types of behavior and then determine what the implications of such behavior are likely to be. This is particularly useful if the exogenous variables can be set as a matter of policy, in which case the forecasts generated by the model can be viewed as educated guesses about the likely effects of exogenous variables taking on certain values.

Clearly these two uses of the forecasts are intertwined, because before policymakers will use a model it must be shown capable of generating accurate forecasts. The model evaluation aspect of forecasting serves such a purpose. Once the model has "passed" this stage, it is a candidate for use by policymakers in playing out the implications of alternative policies.

In order to be able to utilize forecasts in the above two ways, the data involved must be divided into two distinct sets—specifically, into sample (consisting of T observations) and post sample (consisting of m observations) sets. Although the practice of withholding data from a sample has been criticized (e.g., Christ, 1966:546-548), it has also been argued (Dhrymes et al., 1972:306-308) that:

> in a realistic situation in which model selection procedures, hypothesis tests of various kinds, and a number of other "experiments" all amount to a considerable data mining, it would seem wise to have saved some data on which to evaluate the resulting model . . . if the model passes

its predictive test evaluation the m saved observations should then . . . be incorporated into the data set to reestimate the model on all (T + m) observations. If the model fails, then, of course it is back to the "drawing board."

If the model in question passes the evaluation portion of the forecasting enterprise (i.e., if its forecasts can be shown to be sufficiently accurate), the two data sets will then be combined into a single data set consisting of T + m observations. The model parameters can then be re-estimated, and the revised model used to generate forecasts into the blind future.

Given the above distinction, it is clear that two types of forecasts will have to be utilized. The first, hereafter referred to as *ex post* forecasts, are a series of forecasts of the m non-sample data points. Specifically, they are forecasts of the m data points which have been purposely withheld from the sample. The second, hereafter referred to as *ex ante* forecasts, are a series of forecasts into the blind future. These are forecasts of values of the variables which have not yet occurred and which are based on the re-estimated model.

To summarize, the ex post forecasts are of use in the evaluation stage of the forecast enterprise, that is, they are used to evaluate the ability of the estimated model to generate accurate forecasts of the variables of interest. If it can be shown that the model is capable of accurate forecasts, then a series of ex ante forecasts can be used to provide educated guesses about the path of the variables into the blind future. Note that just because a model does well in one type of forecasting does not mean that it will do well in the other. All that we can do is hope that this is the case.

In the remainder of this section, we will focus on the reasons why all forecasts contain error. Having established the reasons for this error, the manner in which the forecasts are to be generated will be discussed in some detail. Next, the topic of forecast evaluation will be discussed and an example will be presented. Finally, ex ante forecasting will be presented and an example will be worked out.

FORECAST ERROR

All forecasts can be expected to contain some error. The reasons for this can be seen by considering a simple forecasting problem. Suppose we have the following model:

$$Y_t = a + bX_t + e_t \quad t = 1, 2, \ldots, T \qquad [68]$$

We can use this knowledge of the past to extrapolate into the future. Thus a reasonable predictor for Y_{T+1} (i.e., the first post sample value) would be its expected value

$$E[Y_{T+1}] = \hat{a} + \hat{b} \; X_{T+1} \qquad [69]$$

The actual value of Y_{T+1} will differ from $E [Y_{T+1}]$ for the following two reasons: first, the random disturbance component of the forecast, e_{T+1}; and second, the sample regression line is not identical to the population regression line because of sampling error. Kmenta (1971:240) has expressed the difference between the actual and forecasted values of the dependent variable, hereafter called *forecast error,* as follows:

$$Y_{T+1} - \hat{Y}_{T+1} = (a + bX_{T+1} + e_{T+1}) - (\hat{a} + \hat{b}X_{T+1}) \qquad [70]$$

This error can be shown to be a normally distributed random variable with a mean of zero and the following variance (Kmenta, 1971:240):

$$s_F^2 = s^2 \left[1 + \frac{1}{T} + \frac{(X_{T+1} - \bar{X})^2}{\sum_t (X_t - \bar{X})^2} \right] \qquad [71]$$

where s_F^2 is the forecast variance, s^2 is the sample variance, X_{T+1} is the post sample value of the exogenous variable, and T is the size of the sample. This means that the forecast error will be smaller (Kmenta, 1971:241): (1) the larger the sample size, (2) the greater the dispersion of the explanatory variable, and (3) the smaller the distance between X_{T+1} and $\bar{X}$. Kmenta (1971: 241) goes on to note that

> The first two conclusions are quite straightforward; they reflect the fact that the better the estimate of the population regression line, the smaller the variance of the forecast error. The third conclusion is more interesting; it means that our forecast will be better for values of X_{T+1} which are closer to $\bar{X}$ than those which are farther away from $\bar{X}$. This is consistent with the intuitively plausible contention that we are better able to forecast within our range of experience than outside of it. In this case the range of our experience is represented by the sample values of the explanatory variable X, and the central point of that range is $\bar{X}$. The farther away we venture with our forecasting, the less reliable the forecast.

In the bivariate relationship, the nature of the forecast error can be seen in Figure 13. For values of X_{T+1} near the sample mean, the width between the error bands is minimal. As the points become more distant from the mean, the band width becomes larger.

It is possible to use knowledge of the forecast error to make probability statements about the forecasts that have been generated. Given that the forecast error is normally distributed, has a zero mean, and has its variance s_F^2, it follows that

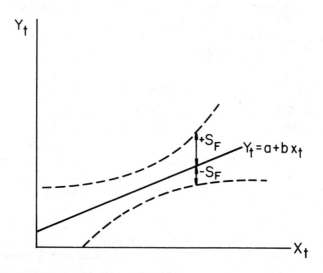

Figure 13: Standard Error of Forecast
Source: Klein (1974, p. 261).

$$\frac{Y_{T+1} - \hat{Y}_{T+1}}{s_F} \sim t_{T-2} \qquad [72]$$

This makes it possible to make probability statements about the forecasts, that is, we can construct a confidence interval around the forecast which will contain the actual value of Y_{T+1} a given percentage of the time. This interval is

$$\hat{Y}_{T+1} \pm t_{T-2} s_F \qquad [73]$$

where t_{T-2} is the t-value taken from a standard table, with T−2 degrees of freedom. This forecast interval can be interpreted just as the usual confidence interval; the interval in equation 73 will contain the actual value some percentage of the time as determined by the level chosen in selecting the t-value.

Therefore it is possible to generate forecasts. These forecasts will contain a certain amount of error coming from two distinct sources. The magnitude of the error can be estimated and forecast intervals can be constructed.

At this point, it seems wise to raise the distinction between point and interval forecasts. A point forecast is a single valued prediction of a variable. An interval forecast provides an interval in which one can expect to find the actual value a fixed proportion of the time. Following Christ (1966:543), we will concentrate on point forecasts because of the fact that single values are easier to work with and are more useful to policymakers. Having indicated how the interval forecast can be computed, we will now concentrate on the generation and evaluation of point forecasts. (If interested in pursuing interval forecasting in more detail, see Kmenta (1971) or Klein (1974).)

FORECAST GENERATION

As might be expected, the best way to generate point forecasts is to use

$$Y_{T+i} = \hat{a} + \hat{b}X_{T+i} + e_{T+i} \qquad [74]$$

where $\hat{a}$ and $\hat{b}$ are the best estimators available under our assumptions, and where e_{T+i} is assumed to have a zero mean, constant variance, and be serially independent. Then the predictor of Y_{T+i} (i.e., $\hat{a} + \hat{b}X_{T+i}$), when $\hat{a}$ and $\hat{b}$ are the appropriate least squares estimators, is a best linear unbiased predictor. This, according to Theil (1971:123), means that "the prediction error of any other predictor of y which is also linear in y and unbiased has a larger prediction error."

The major exception to this extension of the general linear model occurs when the disturbances are not serially independent. When there is serial correlation, prediction will be affected in a nontrivial manner. Specifically, as Johnston (1972:246) argues, the predictions will be inefficient—"that is, predictions with needlessly large sampling variances" will result. Serial correlation in the prediction context can be dealt with just as it can be in the sample. When e_{T+i} is correlated with e_{T+i-1}, any predictor which ignores the error can be improved upon. For example, consider the following model:

$$Y_{T+i} = a + bX_{T+i} + e_{T+i}$$
$$e_{T+i} = pe_{T+i-1} + v_{T+i} \qquad [75]$$

where v_{T+i} meets all of the usual assumptions. Klein (1974:271) suggests two alternative formulations for forecasting with serially correlated error terms. The first involves substituting each separate period for the disturbance term. From equation 75 we know

$$e_{T+i} = p(Y_{T+i-1} - a - bX_{T+i-1}) + v_{T+i} \qquad [76]$$

by substitution for e_{T+i-1}. Then Y_{T+i} can be expressed as

$$Y_{T+i} = a(1-p) + bX_{T+i} - bpX_{T+i-1} + pY_{T+i-1} + v_{T+i} \qquad [77]$$

We can then assume v_{T+i} to take on its expected value, zero, and then use the following equation to generate the forecast:

$$Y_{T+i} = a(1-p) + bX_{T+i} - bpX_{T+i-1} + p\dot{Y}_{T+i-1} \qquad [78]$$

where

$$\dot{Y}_{T+i-1} = a(1-p) + bX_{T+i-1} - bpX_{T+i-1} + p\dot{Y}_{T+i-2}$$

As can be seen, we must estimate the lagged endogenous variable since we do not usually know its exact values. Thus, in addition to the usual sources of forecast error, we must allow for variability in $\dot{Y}_{T+i-j}$. This change makes the computation of the standard error of the forecast much more complicated (Klein, 1974:268). The problems which have been discussed in the context of estimating the lagged endogenous variable do not arise for single period forecasts, however, because the values of the lagged endogenous variable are presumably known. Problems do arise if we generate forecasts more than one period into the future.

As a second method of generating forecasts, Klein (1974:271) suggests simply disregarding serial correlation in the post sample period. Forecasting from the previous equation involves the use of longer lags than in the serially uncorrelated case, so there may be error accumulation due to incorporating assumptions about the behavior of the error term. Thus Klein (1974) concludes that it is not obvious that the first forecasting approach is going to perform better than

$$Y_{T+i} = \hat{a} + \hat{b}X_{T+i} + 0 \qquad [79]$$

where a and b are GLS estimates of the parameters and the error term is assumed to be zero.

We are therefore faced with a dilemma if, when generating point forecasts, there are serially correlated errors in the sample period. This dilemma concerns the method to be used to generate the forecasts. There are essentially two different approaches, and while there is no clear evidence as to which is better, it seems reasonable to use the first procedure, because it includes some consideration of the serial correlation.

MODIFYING THE FORECASTING EQUATION

It should now be clear that numerical values for the forecasts can be obtained based on the sample period parameter estimates. The point of the present discussion, however, is to suggest that there may be times when we wish to be a bit less mechanical in our approach to forecast generation. Klein (1974:278-279), for example, argues quite persuasively that there is considerable room for judgment and insight in the generation of forecasts:

> It is a fact of life that purely numerical methods cannot be used, but must be supplemented by special information and personal judgment. . . . The objectively estimated model is needed as a framework in which to interpret the special and subjective information.

This section provides an objective technique with which to generate forecasts, but the forecaster must be ready to supplement mechanics with insights into the problem at hand. As Klein (1974:279) cautions:

The use of econometric results should be as quantitative as possible, but attempts at pure push button mechanistic uses are sure to fail and prove inferior to methods that combine formal estimated model with a priori information (qualitative as well as quantitative) and judgment. Economic prediction has been rendered less of an art and more of a science by the use of econometric methods but it has not been reduced to a pure scientific exercise.

With these warnings in mind, we will now consider how to incorporate information based on our insight and judgment into the forecast generation.

Depending upon the type of information we possess, numerous factors can be introduced into the forecast generation. One important type of information concerns the specific form of the forecasting equation. Is the same structure that was operating in the sample period likely to remain in force during the post sample period? If so, the estimated equation can be used as is. If not, it may be necessary to change the sign and/or magnitude of one or more of the parameters. In addition, it may be necessary to drop or add variables to the relationship in order to account for drastic changes in the environment (e.g., war or the development of a new type of weapon): if, in the context of our ongoing example, we knew that the U.S. had altered its ratio goal, we could simply change the value of that parameter before generating the forecasts.

A second type of modification concerns the manner in which the disturbances are used; the issue revolves around whether we wish to formally acknowledge the impact of v_{T+i} on the forecast by adding a random variable to each forecast. Since we usually have no information with which to make such an addition, the general practice is to ignore the error term and generate the forecasts as if the equation were deterministic: this is called *nonstochastic* forecasting. If, however, the disturbance term variance is known, it may be possible to draw estimated disturbance terms from an estimated probability distribution and then add that to each forecast—this is called *stochastic* forecasting. In equation 74, for example, we could assume either that the value of each e_{T+i} is zero or that the value of e_{T+i} can be estimated and added to each forecast.

A third type of modification concerns the generation of forecasts in which the values of the exogenous variables are not known. In such instances we may wish to devise a rule for estimating these values. For example, we could assume that the variable follows a first order autoregressive process and generate the values as follows:

$$\hat{X}_{T+i} = b^i X_T \hspace{3cm} [80]$$

We could then use the estimated values of the exogenous variables in forecasts which would be *conditional* upon specific values of the exogenous variables.

These are just three examples of the manner in which the forecast generating equations can be supplemented by the forecaster. No matter what type of information we have about the process being modeled, every attempt should be made to incorporate it into the forecasts so that as much information as possible is brought to bear on the problem.

FORECAST EVALUATION

In the first part of this section we shall be concerned with the evaluation of ex post forecasts. If the model in question passes this stage of the evaluation enterprise, it is then possible to generate ex ante forecasts, which will be discussed in turn.

Before moving on to an explicit consideration of forecast accuracy, however, it is necessary to make the following specification. When we are speaking of ex post forecasts we will use the notation

$$Y_{T+i} = a + bX_{T+i} \qquad [81]$$

whereas for ex ante forecasts the form will be

$$Y_{T+m+j} = a + bX_{T+m+j} \qquad [82]$$

where

$t = 1, 2, \ldots, T$ sample
$i = 1, 2, \ldots, m$ post sample (available but not included in sample)
$j = 1, 2, \ldots, n$ not available at present time

To this point, we have discussed the generation of point forecasts: it is now necessary to evaluate the accuracy of such forecasts. Such an evaluation is important, both because it is wise to have an idea about the "average" magnitude of the forecast error and because it provides a basis from which to determine whether or not that magnitude is acceptable.

The assessment of the magnitude of forecast error—that is, of the difference between the forecast (P_t) and the actual realization (A_t)—proceeds from an examination of a simple scatter known as a prediction-realization diagram (Theil, 1966:19-26). With the levels of the actual realization and the model forecasts as the axes, the T forecast/realization pairs (P_t, A_t) can be plotted; as a point of reference, a line of perfect forecasts connects those points where the forecasts and the realization would be identical ($P_t = A_t$). A prediction-realization diagram is shown in Figure 14. The smaller the dispersion of the T forecast/realization pairs around the line of perfect forecasts, the more accurate the forecasts. A measure of this dispersion can therefore serve as an absolute measure of forecast accuracy. One such measure, the standard

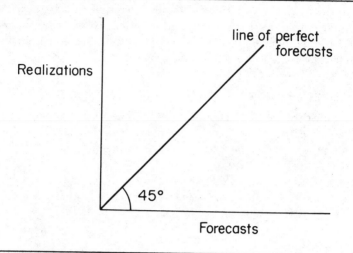

Figure 14: Prediction-Realization Diagram

deviation around the line of perfect forecasts, is the root mean square error of the forecast, $RMSE_f$ (Klein, 1974:442-444):

$$RMSE_f = [T^{-1} \Sigma (P_t - A_t)^2]^{\frac{1}{2}} \qquad [83]$$

where P_t is the model forecast, A_t is the actual realization, and T is the number of forecasts (i.e., t = 1, 2, . . . , T). The $RMSE_f$ measures the average dispersion around the line of perfect forecasts in the same units as the actual realization.

Thus far, our assessment of the short term forecast accuracy has considered a single descriptive measure. Since it is a non-parametric measure, there are no objective standards (e.g., significance levels) with which to assess the forecast accuracy. A determination of the accuracy of the model forecasts can be made, however, by comparing their accuracy to that of a mechanistic alternative—one which requires no prior theorizing (in the sense of having a prior conception of the dynamics of the policymaking process). Such an alternative should be relatively simple, quick, and require no more than some knowledge of the recent history of the endogenous variable.

One such alternative is the naive model test which, according to Christ (1966:572), is a test

consisting of essentially comparing errors of prediction made by a model with those by a "naive model." That is, by a very simple hypothesis set up as a straw man to see if a model can knock it down.

Only if the model in question can "knock down" the naive model will its forecasts be classified as adequate. Specifically, the no-change naive model will be used; this model sets this period's value equal to last period's value plus a random normal disturbance term with a zero mean and a constant but unknown variance:

$$Y_{T+i} = Y_{T+i-1} + u_{T+i}$$

Ignoring the error term, the naive model forecast becomes

$$Y_{T+i} = Y_{T+i-1} \qquad [84]$$

While in no sense an optimal forecasting model, this does provide a convenient and easy baseline criterion for discarding inadequate forecasts.

Although such a comparison does not allow conclusive results, it is a test of the hypothesis that the model in question produces sufficiently accurate forecasts. As Friedman (1951:109) notes:

The reasons can be easily seen. The essential objective behind the derivation of econometric models is to construct a hypothesis of economic change; any econometric model implictly contains a theory of economic change. Now given the existence of economic change, the crucial question is whether the theory implicit in the econometric model abstracts any of the essential forces responsible for economic changes that actually occur. Is it better, that is, than a theory which says there are no forces making for change? Now Naive Model I [equation 84], which says the value of each variable next year will be identical with its value this year, is precisely such a theory; it denies, as it were, the existence of any forces making for change from one year to the next. . . . If the econometric model does no better than this naive model, the implication is that it does not abstract any of the essential forces making for change, that it is of zero value as a theory explaining year to year change.

By substituting "defense expenditure" (or any other term) for "economic" in this statement, it becomes a very powerful and articulate claim for the usefulness of the proposed naive model test. It must be reiterated, however, that the naive model is neither a serious forecasting technique nor a competing theory of policymaking behavior. Its function is simply to provide a standard of comparison—a zero point—below which the model forecasts are inadequate.

Having generated the forecasts and measured their accuracy, the efficiency of the model relative to the naive or benchmark model is determine using the accuracy ratio:

$$\frac{RMSE_{model}}{RMSE_{naive}} \qquad \qquad [85]$$

A value of less than 1.00 indicates that the forecast error in the model under evaluation is less than that of the naive model. A determination of relative accuracy can then be made as follows: (1) if the accuracy ratio is less than 1.00, the model under investigation is more accurate than the naive model; and (2) if the accuracy ratio is greater than or equal to 1.00, the model is inaccurate relative to the naive model.

If the forecasts of a model have been shown to be accurate, the model can be tentatively identified as an acceptable forecasting model. Note that any number of other types of evaluation could be substituted for the naive model. For example we could evaluate the accuracy of a model relative to a contending or alternative theoretical model. Whatever the criteria, once a model is identified as tentatively acceptable as a forecasting tool, it can be used to indicate the future course of the endogenous variable or to ascertain what policy changes that variable might bring about in terms of alternative futures. This procedure is called ex ante forecasting.

In the course of generating and evaluating ex post forecasts, we will use both the ratio goal (equation 1) and revised ratio goal (equation 67) models. The ex post forecast evaluation will attempt to determine the accuracy of both models in terms of 1970-1973 forecasts of the U.S. defense expenditure total. In the course of generating the forecasts, we will employ the method which takes the serial correlation explicitly into account—that is, the forecasts will be generated according to the manner suggested in equation 78. Note that the lagged endogenous variables do not have to be estimated, because their values are already known.

Prior to comparing the performance of the two models, let us compute the 1970-1973 ex post forecasts for equation 1 based on the OLS and pseudo-GLS parameter estimates. The results are presented in Table 7. As can be seen, the version using the OLS parameter estimates is the least efficient, followed by the versions using first differences, Cochrane-Orcutt, and Hildreth-Lu techniques respectively. This is just as would be expected, based on the development of the second section of this paper. Employing GLS and making use of the serial correlation of the estimated residuals yields more accurate forecasts of the 1970-1973 U.S. defense expenditure totals.

Turning to the comparison of the forecasting accuracy of equations 1 and 67, the forecasts and RMSEs are displayed in Table 8. As can be seen by using the RMSE measure, equation 1 is marginally more accurate than equation 67; however, it should be stressed that the differences are not all that great. At the far right hand side of Table 8 are the ex post forecasts of the naive model, which represent a substantial improvement, in terms of RMSE, over the two

TABLE 7
Ex Post Forecast Accuracy of Equation 1
for Alternative Methods of Estimation

Year	Actual Value	Method of Estimation			
		OLS	Cochrane-Orcutt	Hildreth-Lu	First Differences
1970	77150	79030	80288	79723	80994
1971	75546	80832	78500	77921	78962
1972	75084	82471	76936	76486	77281
1973	76435	85748	77228	76962	77204
RMSE	——	6571	2383	1904	2822

versions of the ratio goal model. If we take the previously cited Friedman argument very seriously, neither model appears to "abstract any of the essential forces making for change" in the U.S. defense expenditure policymaking process; hence we might conclude that they are both of "zero value as a theory explaining year to year change" (Friedman, 1951:109).

Thus neither model is especially valuable as a forecast generator. While there are no doubt other ways in which to evaluate the two models, the forecast evaluation has proved to be especially useful. We should also keep in mind the fact that the naive model is not very helpful in generating ex ante

TABLE 8
Ex Post Forecast Accuracy of Equations 1 and 67 When
Serial Correlation Has Been Taken into Account

Year	Actual Value	Equation 1	Equation 67	Naive Model
1970	77170	79723	80635	77872
1971	75546	77921	77978	77170
1972	75084	76486	76777	75546
1973	76435	76962	77117	75084
RMSE		1904	2305	1133

forecasts because it depends upon knowing the previous year's expenditure total. In order to illustrate ex ante forecasting, let us therefore ignore the failure of either model to establish itself as an accurate forecasting instrument and move ahead.

Ex ante forecasting requires both that the T sample period observations be combined with the m post sample observations into a single data set of size N, and that the parameters be re-estimated. A series of ex ante forecasts can then be generated. The accuracy of these forecasts cannot be evaluated in terms of the RMSE, however, since they are directed into the blind future. Their credibility rests on the fact that the model has been carefully evaluated prior to being used to generate ex ante forecasts.

In generating the series of ex ante forecasts, an algorithm similar to equation 82 will be used. Since the forecasts are into the unknown future, the value of some of the variables may be unknown, which causes notable differences between this type of forecasting and the ex post forecasts developed earlier. Ex ante forecasts are usually both multiperiod and conditional. A multiperiod forecast uses the forecasted values of the most recent lagged endogenous variables to generate the subsequent period's forecasts. For example, in equation 82, Y_{T+m} would be used to forecast Y_{T+m+1}, Y_{T+m+1} would be used to forecast Y_{T+m+2}, etc. A conditional forecast is qualified by assuming the occurrence of certain external events. In the context of equation 82, the forecasts could be made on the condition that the parameter values do not change their value and that the X_{T+m+j} are known or can be estimated.

A series of scenarios can be devised in which a variety of different combinations of conditions are imposed on equations like 82, in order to ascertain the sensitivity of the model to a range of hypothetical situations. From each scenario an alternative future time path for the endogenous variables can be generated. If the scenarios cover a large enough number of possibilities, the alternative futures will probably provide a range within which the policymaker can expect to find the endogenous variables in the future. Furthermore, if a policy is defined as a particular set of specific parameter values, this type of analysis will also allow the policymaker to determine the effect of policy changes or to ascertain what changes will be required to bring about specific future values of the current endogenous variables.

In the course of generating such ex ante forecasts, we will make use of the following two scenarios:

Scenario 1: $X_{T+m} = \$94$ billion

$$X_{T+m+j} = 1.04^j X_{T+m+j-1}$$

Scenario 2: $X_{T+m} = \$94$ billion

$$X_{T+m+j} = 1.10^j X_{T+m+j-1}$$

In Scenario 1, we are acknowledging two factors. First, recent estimates of USSR defense spending suggest that, as of 1973 or 1974, the USSR is spending in excess of $90 billion. Compared to data used to estimate equations 1 and 67, this represents a jump of approximately $30 billion over the course of a single year. Second, we are assuming that, once this change of base is taken into account, the USSR defense expenditure total will continue to grow at the rate of four percent per year (which, incidentally, is its historical growth rate). In Scenario 2, we are making the same first assumption but altering the second. Specifically, we are assuming that USSR defense expenditures are going to rise at the rate of ten percent per year over the next seven years. This is probably the upper bound at which one could picture USSR spending changing.

Prior to generating the ex ante forecasts, the sample and post sample data sets are combined and the models estimate using T+m or 20 data points. The two equations are then estimated using the Hildreth-Lu and IV-GLS techniques, respectively. The revised estimates are given in Table 9, and show that the relative status of the two models in terms of the usual goodness of fit indicators remains the same.

The ex ante forecasts are generated using the format discussed in equation 78, and are displayed in Table 10 according to the expected USSR expendi-

TABLE 9
Pseudo-GLS Estimates for Equations 1 and 67
When 1954-1973 Data is Used

Equation 1

$$Y_t = 3223 + .744 \ X_t$$
$$(0.16) \quad (2.28)$$

$$R^2 = .31 \qquad s.e. = 4320$$
$$DW = 1.11 \qquad N = 19$$

Equation 67

$$Y_t = 1705 + .532 \ Y_{t-1} + .551 \ X_t$$
$$(0.59) \quad (2.89) \qquad (1.00)$$

$$R^2 = .73 \qquad s.e. = 3706$$
$$h = 1.99 \qquad N = 19$$

TABLE 10
Ex Ante Forecasts by Equations 1 and 67 for Scenarios 1 and 2

Year	Equation 1		Equation 67	
	Scenario 1	Scenario 2	Scenario 1	Scenario 2
1974	89733	89733	90213	90213
1975	96992	101469	100873	104060
1976	104045	113780	110659	119144
1977	110936	126784	119434	134810
1978	117700	140604	127332	150975
1979	124373	155370	134566	167797
1980	127844	171219	141343	185525

ture totals. Since the actual data do not exist, it is impossible to investigate the absolute accuracy of these forecasts, but they are nevertheless displayed in Figure 15 in order to suggest the manner in which they might be used. This plot should provide the bounds within which we can expect to find the U.S. defense expenditure total over the next few years. (Given the lack of

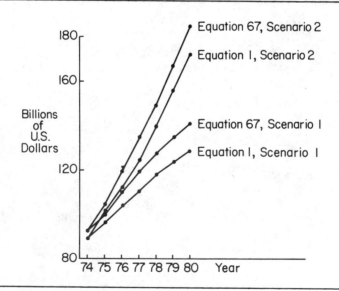

Figure 15: Ex Ante Forecasts

success both in the estimation and in the ex post forecasting phases of the analysis, however, we do not of course place much credence in the actual values displayed either in Table 10 or in Figure 15.)

It has been shown that even though a model's functional form has been correctly specified and its parameters have been properly estimated, it may not be able to generate accurate forecasts. An evaluation procedure has therefore been proposed which uses the model to elicit enough explicit information so that its forecasting accuracy can be assessed. Furthermore, once the model has been identified as tentatively acceptable in terms of the accuracy of its forecasts, a wealth of policy-relevant information can be generated through the process of ex ante forecasting. It must be noted that the identification of the model as tentatively acceptable does not necessarily guarantee that its ex ante forecasts will be admissible.

5. ALTERNATIVE TIME-DEPENDENT PROCESSES

To this point, we have assumed that the time-dependent process generating the error terms can be represented adequately by a first order autoregressive model. The basic justification for this assumption has been given by Theil (1971:251):

The idea underlying such a process is that the neglected variables which are represented by the disturbance move gradually over time. It is then plausible that successive disturbances e_t and e_{t-1} are positively correlated, that the correlation of more distant disturbances is closer to zero than that of e_t and e_{t-1}, and that the correlation converges toward zero when the distance in time becomes larger and larger.

It has been shown in a previous section that this describes the behavior of disturbance terms generated by a first order autoregressive process. It is now reasonable to inquire whether the first order autoregressive process is appropriate for all disturbance processes. As noted in an earlier section, the first order autoregressive process is merely a crude approximation, nothing more. Almost all treatments of autoregressive disturbances focus on the first order process, because of its tractability. Consequently, few are aware of the possibility that some other process might be generating the disturbances.

The decision as to which time-dependent process is responsible for the errors is an important one because, as Hibbs (1974:296) points out, "the desirable properties of GLS are not in general preserved if the time-dependent process is incorrectly specified—indeed, the investigator who proceeds on the basis of a misspecified process may do more damage than good." How then can we identify the correct process? While there is no way we can be sure what process is generating the errors, it is possible to use the estimated residuals to identify the type and the parameters of the process generating those residuals.

The concept of the autocorrelation function and correlogram has already been discussed in order to illustrate what the first order autoregressive process implies about the correlation of the residuals. Figures 7 and 8 provide a plot of the autocorrelation functions for positive and negative first order autoregressive processes. Hibbs (1974) presents a very convincing case for the role of the correlogram in characterizing the disturbances of a particular regression model. The idea is to apply OLS to the original model and obtain the residuals. The residuals can then be used to estimate the autocorrelation function and correlogram. The empirical correlogram is then compared to theoretical correlograms of various possible disturbance-generating processes. Note that the first order autoregressive process is but one possible model which could be responsible for the serially correlated residuals. In the following section, we will examine the theoretical correlograms of a number of time-dependent processes.

The topics we are about to discuss are somewhat more advanced than most of the previous discussion, but it is important to be aware of some of the different processes which might be generating the residuals. Higher order autoregressive, moving average, mixed autoregressive/moving average models will all be explored as possible candidates. Because of their great flexibility in accounting for a wide range of autocorrelation functions and therefore for a wide range of disturbance term behavior, these processes constitute a powerful class of disturbance term models.

THE ALTERNATIVE PROCESSES

In this section, we will explore the three types of processes that could be generating serially correlated error terms. Each type of process and its implications in terms of the autocorrelation function will be explored in turn.

Higher Order Autoregressive Processes

Having already looked at the first order autoregressive process in great detail (equation 10), we will consider the possibility that the residuals are generated by a higher order autoregressive process. It could be, for example, that the current disturbance is made up of portions of the previous two disturbances. This would be consistent with a second order autoregressive model, AR(2), and can be formalized as:

$$e_t = p_1 e_{t-1} + p_2 e_{t-2} + v_t \qquad [86]$$

$$p_1 + p_2 < 1$$

$$p_2 - p_1 < 1$$

$$-1 < p_2 < 1$$

$$E[e_t] = E[v_t] = E[e_{t-i}v_t] = 0 \qquad i \neq 0$$

$$E[v_t^2] = \sigma^2$$

$$E[v_t v_{t-i}] = 0 \qquad i \neq 0$$

The autocorrelation function of the AR(2) process is as follows:

$$A_1 = p_1/1 - p_2 \qquad\qquad [86]$$

$$A_2 = p_2 + (p_1^2/1 - p_2) \qquad\qquad [87]$$

$$A_j = p_1 A_{j-1} + p_2 A_{j-2} \quad j > 2 \qquad\qquad [88]$$

Figure 16 presents hypothetical correlograms for various combinations of the parameters p_1 and p_2. Note how the correlograms in Figure 16 contrast with those of the AR(1) process depicted in Figures 7 and 8. It should be clear that an AR(2) process can yield a variety of alternative correlograms depending upon the values of the two parameters.

The autocorrelation function for higher order autoregressive processes follows relatively straightforwardly from the above development. There are k equations that together determine the first k values of the autocorrelation function (Pindyck and Rubinfield, 1976:464-465):

$$A_1 = p_1 + p_2 A_1 + \ldots + p_k A_{k-1}$$

$$\vdots$$

$$A_k = p_1 A_{k-1} + p_2 A_{k-2} + \ldots + p_k$$

For displacements greater than k periods, the following autocorrelations should hold:

$$A_j = p_1 A_{j-1} + p_2 A_{j-2} + \ldots + p_k A_{j-k} \quad j > k \qquad\qquad [91]$$

These general expressions can be used to deduce the empirical behavior of disturbances generated by an autoregressive process of degree k.

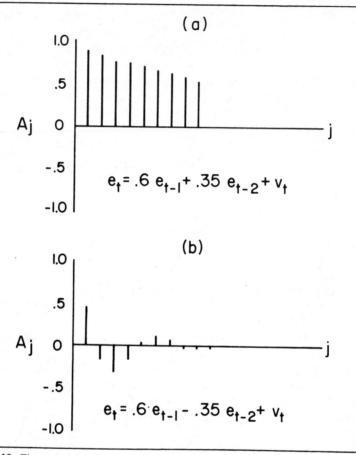

(a)

$$e_t = .6\, e_{t-1} + .35\, e_{t-2} + v_t$$

(b)

$$e_t = .6\, e_{t-1} - .35\, e_{t-2} + v_t$$

Figure 16: Theoretical Correlograms for AR(2) Disturbance Processes

Moving Average Processes

In a moving average process, the pattern of disturbances is described completely by a weighted sum of current and lagged random disturbances. The disturbances are the result of the factors discussed in the second section of this monograph. If these disturbances have both an immediate effect on the dependent variable and a discounted effect over time, and if the discounting is such that the disturbances exert an influence up to q periods after its occurrence, then a moving average process of order q, MA(q), may be an appropriate model for the time-dependent process. The moving average process of order q is given by the following equation:

$$e_t = v_t - d_1 v_{t-1} - d_2 v_{t-2} - \ldots - d_q v_{t-q} \qquad [92]$$

where the parameters, d_i, can be either positive or negative. The random disturbances are generated in such a way that each v_t has a zero mean, constant variance, and zero autocorrelation. In contrast to the AR(k) models, a moving average process is the product of random shock, which occurs and disturbs the dependent variable for some fixed number of periods before disappearing. The autocorrelation function produced by a MA(q) model will, therefore, differ sharply from that of a AR(k) model.

To see this, consider the first order moving average model, MA(1):

$$e_t = v_t - d_1 v_{t-1} \qquad [93]$$

where

$$-1 < d_1 < 1$$

$$E[e_t] = E[v_t] = E[e_{t-i}v_t] = E[v_t v_{-i}] = 0 \qquad i \neq 0$$

$$E[v_t^2] = \sigma^2$$

In the first order moving average process, the effect is to "forget" what happened more than one period in the past. That is, random shocks are totally discounted after a lag of one period. The autocorrelation function of such a process is given by:

$$A_1 = -d_1/1 + d_1^2$$
$$A_j = 0 \qquad j > 1 \qquad [94]$$

Thus the autocorrelation function of the MA(1) process should be zero for all but the single period lag. This produces a correlogram which is easily distinguished from the AR(1) correlograms presented earlier. Examples of MA(1) processes are presented in Figure 17.

Second and higher order moving average processes follow straightforwardly from the first order model. The second order moving average process, MA(2), is given by

$$e_t = v_t - d_1 v_{t-1} - d_2 v_{t-2} \qquad [95]$$

where the terms have been defined previously. In the MA(2) model, the random shocks are completely discounted after two periods. The autocorrelation function for the MA(2) model is given by:

$$A_1 = -d_1(1-d_2)/(1 + d_1^2 + d_2^2) \qquad [96]$$

$$A_2 = -d_2/(1 + d_1^2 + d_2^2) \qquad [97]$$

$$A_j = 0 \qquad\qquad j > 2 \qquad [98]$$

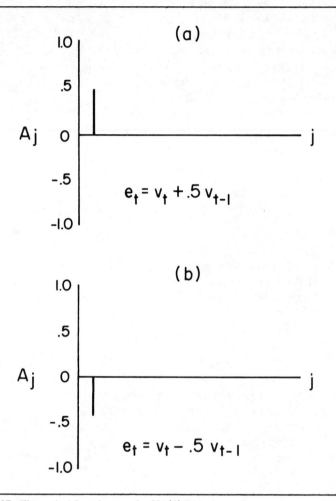

Figure 17: Theoretical Correlograms for MA(1) Disturbance Processes

Thus the autocorrelation function of a MA(2) process should show correlations at the first two lags and zero correlation thereafter. Examples of MA(2) process correlograms are presented in Figure 18.

Finally, the general form of the MA(q) process is given by the following autocorrelation function.

$$A_j = \frac{-d_j + d_1 d_{j+1} + \ldots + d_{q-j} d_q}{1 + d_1^2 + d_2^2 + \ldots + d_q^2} \qquad j = 1, \ldots, q \qquad [99]$$

$$A_j = 0 \qquad\qquad\qquad\qquad j > q$$

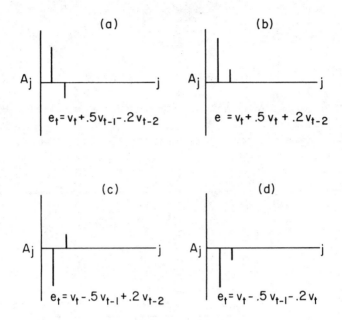

Figure 18: Theoretical Correlograms for MA(2) Disturbance Processes

The hallmark of the autocorrelation function of an MA(q) process is non-zero correlation at lags 1 through q and zero correlations elsewhere.

Mixed Processes

In addition to the AR(k) and MA(q) processes, it is possible that the errors could follow a pattern made up of both types of processes. Such a mixed process, usually referred to as ARMA(k,q), do not have an easy interpretation. For the most part an ARMA model is employed on the grounds of parsimony (it requires that fewer parameters be estimated); an ARMA(k,q) process can be approximated by higher order autoregressive or moving average processes (Box and Jenkins, 1970).

The simplest mixed process is one which combines the first order autoregressive and moving average models. Such a model, ARMA(1,1) can be formalized as:

$$e_t = p_1 e_{t-1} + v_t - d_1 v_{t-1} \qquad [100]$$

The autocorrelation function for this process is given by

$$A_1 = \frac{(1 - p_1 d_1)(p_1 - d_1)}{1 + d_1^2 - 2p_1 d_1} \qquad [101]$$

$$A_j = p_1 A_{j-1} \qquad\qquad j > 2 \qquad [102]$$

An example of ARMA(1,1) autocorrelation function is given in Figure 19.

Pindyck and Rubinfeld (1976:467) show that for higher order mixed autoregressive/moving average processes, the variances, covariances and autocorrelation functions are solutions to difference equations that cannot be solved

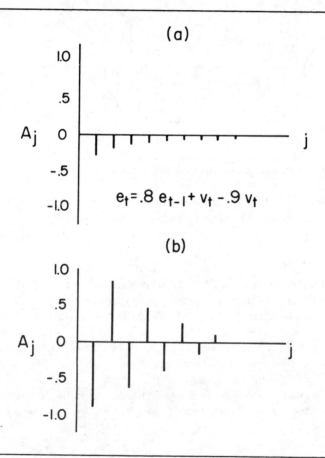

Figure 19: Theoretical Correlograms for ARMA(1,1) Disturbance Processes

by inspection. They do show, however, that we should observe an irregular pattern for q periods, and then the following pattern for lags greater than q:

$$A_j = p_1 A_{j-1} + p_2 A_{j-2} + \cdots + p_k A_{j-k}$$
$$j > q$$

[103]

Since q is the memory of the moving average part of the process, the auto-correlation function exhibits the properties of a pure autoregressive process for lags greater than q.

Given the wide range of processes which could be generating the error terms, we have a great deal of flexibility in terms of characterizing the process that might be responsible for the autocorrelation. Having provided an introduction to a number of different types of processes and having discussed their theoretical correlograms, it is now possible to turn to the identification of such models.

PROCESS IDENTIFICATION

Hibbs (1974:278) argues that the analysis of an empirical correlogram is an effective way to "deduce" the time-dependent process which characterizes the disturbances in individual regression equations. While it is necessary to take issue with the word "deduce," it does seem wise to begin any assessment of possible autocorrelation by looking at the empirical correlogram. Thus we should first estimate the equation with OLS, retrieve the estimated residuals, and use them to estimate the correlogram. The correlogram can then be compared to a variety of theoretical correlograms to find an appropriate model for the disturbance time-dependent process; on the basis of this information an informed specification of the process can be made.

It should be stressed at this point that the procedure about to be outlined can be carried to extremes. There is no mechanical method of discovering the time-dependent process which is responsible for the errors. Instead, the correlogram analysis can be used to make an informed guess in cases where we do not have other a priori information concerning the process. If we have some theoretical reason to suppose a first order process, then we should by all means go ahead with that and avoid the correlogram analysis.

The empirical correlogram is obtained by computing A_j from the OLS residuals, e_t. Thus A_1 is estimated by averaging the correlation of all residuals one period apart; A_2 is estimated by averaging all of the correlations between residuals two periods apart; and so on. It should be clear that there will be a lot more correlations to average for A_1 than for A_3. In fact, there will be only one correlation used to estimate A_{T-1} where T is the sample size. As a consequence, the estimates for longer lagged correlations are likely to be subject to extreme variability. To overcome this problem, the usual prescription is to compute autocorrelations for T/4 or T/5 lags only. For example, we have been using, T = 16; therefore we might compute autocorrelations of lags one, two, three, and four. While this procedure reduces the number of estimated autocorrelations in the correlogram, we can be more confident about those that are included. The best that can be hoped for is that we get a general idea about the pattern of the correlations.

Having estimated the empirical correlogram, it is possible to try to identify the underlying disturbance generating process. Given the previous development, we should make the following decisions:

(1) The residuals are random, if $A_j = 0$ for all $j > 0$.

(2) The residuals are generated by an autoregressive process if they tail off according to equation 91.

(3) The residuals are generated by a moving average process, if A_j has spikes at lags 1 through q and then cuts off entirely.

(4) The residuals are generated by a mixed autoregressive/moving average process, if there is an irregular pattern at lags 1 through q, and then A_j tails off according to equation 103.

These are just simple rules of thumb which one can use to investigate the empirical correlogram. There will be times when it will not be possible to tell for sure what is going on, especially for small samples.

Application to Models with Lagged Endogenous Variables

The procedure which has been outlined in this section is directly applicable to models with lagged endogenous variables with one minor modification: when the model in question has a lagged endogenous variable, it is necessary to use an instrumental variables estimation technique (see third section) to obtain consistent estimates of the residuals. Once the consistent estimates of the residuals have been generated, it is possible to estimate the correlogram and identify the underlying process.

ESTIMATION

Having identified the time-dependent process, it is appropriate to turn to the estimation of the parameters of the process. The estimation of the parameters of the time-dependent process is an extremely difficult enterprise, and is too advanced for inclusion with the present treatment. The interested reader should consult Hibbs (1974); even though his treatment is not complete, he does provide a good overview and bibliography. Once the parameters of the time-dependent process have been estimated, it is a relatively straightforward matter to use them in an application of the pseudo-GLS estimation technique.

6. SUMMARY

In the course of this monograph we have thoroughly explored the realm of time series regression analysis. The presentation has, at times, become quite detailed and mathematical. This was necessary because it is important to understand why we must make transformations and re-estimate models which exhibit problems with serial correlation. The nonautoregression assumption (and hence the time series model) deserves special attention because of the fact that it is so useful in terms of making forecasts and/or evaluating policy. The focus on the nonautoregression assumption is warranted both because of its frequent violation and because of its potentially devastating consequences for substantive inference. If it were just a statistical problem it might not be worth such extensive treatment; however, because its very dramatic implications can be easily remedied, extensive emphasis is likely to be productive. Given that the goal of social science is to make inductive inferences, the consequences of violating the nonautoregression assumption become very important if work is to be cumulative and relevant.

NOTE

1. The following definitions may be of assistance:

Expected Value: The expression $E[e_t]$ should be read as "E of e_t" and not as "E times e_t"; E is an operator and not a quantity. The expectation of e_t is simply the mean of e_t.

Variance: The variance, or $\text{var}(e_t)$ is defined as

$$\text{var}(e_t) = E[(e_t - E(e_t)]^2$$

and is a measure of the spread of a distribution. In terms of the expected value definition, it is the mean of the squared deviations of e_t from $E[e_t]$.

Covariance: The covariance, or $\text{cov}(e_t)$ is defined as

$$\text{cov}(e_t e_{t-m}) = E[(e_t - E(e_t)(e_{t-m} - E(e_{t-m})]$$

and is an indicator of the direction of association between e_t and e_{t-m}.

REFERENCES

BOX, G.E.P. and G. M. JENKINS (1970) Time Series Analysis. San Francisco: Holden-Day.

BUSE, A. (1973) "Goodness of fit in generalized least squares estimation." American Statistician 27:106-109.

CHRIST, C. (1966) Econometric Models and Methods. New York: John Wiley.

DHYRMES, P. J., E. P. HOWREY, S. H. HYMANS, J. KMENTA, E. E. LEAMER, R. E. QUANDT, J. B. RAMSEY, H. T. SHAPIRO, and V. ZARNOWITZ (1972) "Criteria for the evaluation of econometric models." Annals of Economic and Social Measurement 1 (July):259-324.

DURBIN, J. (1970) "Testing for serial correlation in least-squares regression when some of the regressors are lagged dependent variables." Econometrica 38:410-421.

FRIEDMAN, M. (1951) "Comments," pp. 107-114 in National Bureau of Economic Research (ed.) Conference on Business Cycles. New York: National Bureau of Economic Research, Inc.

GRILICHES, Z. (1967) "Distributed lags: a survey." Econometrica 35:16-49.

――― (1961) "A note on the serial correlation bias in estimates of distributed lags." Econometrica 29:65-73.

――― and P. RAO (1969) "Small-sample properties of several two-stage regression methods in the context of autocorrelated errors." Journal of the American Statistical Association 64:253-272.

HABIBAGAHI, H. and J. L. PRATSCHKE (1972) "A comparison of the power of the Von Neumann ratio, Durbin-Watson and Geary tests." Review of Economics and Statistics (May):179-185.

HIBBS, D. (1974) "Problems of statistical estimation and causal inference in dynamic time series models," pp. 252-308 in Herbert Costner (ed.) Sociological Methodology 1973/1974. San Francisco: Jossey-Bass.

JOHNSTON, J. (1972) Econometric Methods. New York: McGraw-Hill.

KELEJIAN, H. H. and W. E. OATES (1974) Introduction to Econometrics: Principles and Applications. New York: Harper & Row.

KLEIN, L. R. (1974) A Textbook of Econometrics. Englewood Cliffs: Prentice-Hall.

――― (1971) An Essay on the Theory of Economic Prediction. Chicago: Markham.

KMENTA, J. (1971) Elements of Econometrics. New York: Macmillan.

MALINVAUD, E. (1970) Statistical Methods of Econometrics. Amsterdam: North-Holland Publishing Co.

NELSON, C. R. (1973) Applied Time Series Analysis. San Francisco: Holden-Day.

NERLOVE, M. and K. F. WALLIS (1966) "Use of the Durbin-Watson statistic in inappropriate situations." Econometrica 34:235-238.

NIE, N. H. et al. (1975) SPSS: Statistical Package for the Social Sciences. New York: McGraw-Hill.

OSTROM, C. W., Jr. (1977) "Evaluating alternative foreign policy decision-making models." Journal of Conflict Resolution 21:235-266.

――― and F. W. HOOLE (forthcoming) "Alliances and wars revisited: a research note." International Studies Quarterly.

PINDYCK, R. S. and D. L. RUBINFELD (1976) Econometric Models and Economic Forecasts. New York: McGraw-Hill.

Princeton University Department of Economics (1974) Time Series Processor User's Manual.

RATTINGER, H. (1975) "Armaments, detente, and bureaucracy." Journal of Conflict Resolution 19:571-595.

RICHARDSON, L. F. (1970) Arms and Insecurity. Pittsburgh: Boxwood.

THEIL, H. (1971) Principles of Econometrics. New York: John Wiley.

——— (1966) Applied Economic Forecasting. Chicago: Rand-McNally.

——— and A. L. Nagar (1961) "Testing the independence of regression disturbances." Journal of the American Statistical Association 56:793-806.

WONNACOTT, R. J. and T. H. WONNACOTT (1970) Econometrics. New York: John Wiley.

CHARLES W. OSTROM, JR. is assistant professor of political science at Michigan State University. He holds a Ph.D. from Indiana University and has authored several papers in the areas of international politics, methodology, and public policy. He is currently doing research in the foreign policy decisionmaking area.

3.00
ch

QUANTITATIVE
APPLICATIONS
IN THE
CIAL SCIENCES

*A SAGE UNIVERSITY
PAPER SERIES*

SPECIAL
OFFER:

4 or more
for $2.50 each
(prepaid only)

meets the need
for brief, clear
explanations of
methodological
techniques—for
those with limited
knowledge of
statistics and
mathematics

improves the quality
of data analysis
in the social
sciences

ideal for use as
classroom
supplements

SAGE PUBLICATIONS
Beverly Hills · London

ORDER CARD

Quantitative Applications
in the Social Sciences

(A Sage University Papers Series)

NAME

ADDRESS

CITY   STATE   ZIP

☐ I want to take advantage of your **Special Offer**. Please send me
the following 4 or more titles at $2.50 each. My check or money
order is enclosed.

☐ **ANALYSIS OF VARIANCE**
(Iversen/Norpoth 407001)
☐ **OPERATIONS RESEARCH METHODS**
(Nagel/Neef 407002)
☐ **CAUSAL MODELING**
(Asher 407003)
☐ **TESTS OF SIGNIFICANCE**
(Henkel 407004)
☐ **COHORT ANALYSIS**
(Glenn 407005)
☐ **CANONICAL ANALYSIS &
FACTOR COMPARISON**
(Levine 407006)
☐ **ANALYSIS OF NOMINAL DATA**
(Reynolds 407007)
☐ **ANALYSIS OF ORDINAL DATA**
(Hildebrand/Lang/Rosenthal 407008)
☐ **TIME SERIES ANALYSIS: Regression Techniques**
(Ostrom 407009)
☐ **ECOLOGICAL INFERENCE**
(Langbein/Lichtman 407010)
☐ **MULTIDIMENSIONAL SCALING**
(Kruskal/Wish 407011)
☐ **ANALYSIS OF COVARIANCE**
(Wildt/Ahtola 407012)
☐ **INTRODUCTION TO FACTOR ANALYSIS**
(Kim/Mueller 407013)
☐ **FACTOR ANALYSIS**
(Kim/Mueller 407014)

☐ Please send me the Sage Papers checked above at the regular
price of $3.00 each.

☐ Payment enclosed $_____

☐ Please bill me $_____*
*plus postage & shipping

| ORDERS FOR |
| $10.00 OR LESS |
| **MUST** BE PREPAID |

(California residents add 6% sales tax)

☐ **Please add my name to your mailing list for announcements of
new titles in this series.**

SAGE Publications, Inc.
P. O. Box 5024 / Beverly Hills, CA 90210

Quantitative Applications
in the Social Sciences

(A Sage University Papers Series)

$3.00 each

PLACE
STAMP
HERE

SAGE PUBLICATIONS, INC.
P. O. Box 5024
BEVERLY HILLS, CALIF. 90210